IN GOOD SPIRITS

David J. Ludwig

Jean —
In appreciation
of your considerable
efforts toward "the Spirit
of God's People." May God
continue to bless your Spirit"
David J. Ludwig
5/4/8

AUGSBURG Publishing House • Minneapolis

CONTENTS

PREFACE

What is a person's spirit? This question has been haunting me ever since I began my work as a therapist. Oh, I could easily tell when people were in good spirits by their enthusiasm, interest and openness to others. And when that spirit had broken down, the depression, heaviness and lack of energy was all too apparent. But just what was this "spirit"?

The first married couple I worked with almost a decade ago gave this concept a concrete focus for me. It was clear that "something was missing" between the two people as they struggled to relate to each other. Almost everything that was said by one was taken "in the wrong spirit," so their communication only led to further hurt and brokenness.

But then, as they were helped to restore contact with each other, something different was present. The mood seemed to shift. What was said was taken in the "right spirit" again, signaling a healthier relationship.

Over the next few years, it dawned on me that this was a spiritual matter! Better contact and a healthier relationship went hand in hand with restoring a good spirit between the two persons. These observations about the "spirit" as it exists between two people became the basis of my first book, *The Spirit of Your Marriage* (Augsburg, 1979).

But even as I wrote that book, I realized that the concept of one's "spirit" went much deeper. And it is to this broader topic that the present book is addressed. Starting from the basic premise that a "spirit" exists between two or more persons and reflects *the quality of their relationship,* this book takes a deep look at a person's "spirits." To be "in good spirits" means that a person's relationships with self, with others, and with God are deep, healthy, and growing.

Therefore, this concept of "spirit" has become for me the intersection point between psychology and the Christian faith. A good spirit is God's gift to us that makes life worth living. But the breakdown of this spirit results in anxiety, depression, loneliness and, finally, hopelessness. This is where bad spirits and "demons" take over a person's life.

I have chosen to use the word *demon* because in classical Greek this word is used to describe deep energy that, when it is not integrated into the total self, has the power to control the whole personality. My use of the term does not imply a being that comes in from the outside to control the person. Rather this term expresses the result of blocked energy or misdirected emotion within relationships. A demon, in my use of the word, is the person's own misdirected energy (like hatred) that has taken a destructive path. The word expresses both the power and the impersonality of this energy as it further destroys one's relationships.

The Christian message is one of reconciliation—the restoration of relationships, the re-creation of one's spirits. God's forgiveness through Jesus Christ—the power for reconciliation—is made real for us through the Holy Spirit. "Oh, to be in good spirits" is the yearning of all God's people as we pray: "Create in me a clean heart, O God, and put a new and right spirit within me" (Ps. 51:10).

This book is dedicated to my wife, Kathy, and our three sons, Tim, Dan, and Mike, who are all deeply a part of my good spirits. I give special thanks to Bryce Thomas for his many insightful comments as the book neared completion.

PART ONE
WHAT ARE THESE GOOD SPIRITS?

These first three chapters present a basic definition of *spirit* as the quality of a relationship. These chapters look at human nature and the potential God has placed in the soul for the formation of these relationships. How these relationships form the basis of a person's "spiritual life" gives this phrase new meaning in our age.

1

What Is It Like

to Be in Good Spirits?

Kathy was still half asleep, wondering why the alarm had not gone off. She was about ready to jump out of bed and wake everyone up when she realized it was Saturday. So she settled back in bed, lazily thinking about the coming weekend. *Get everyone busy around the house this morning, and then we can all have time for tennis, sunning—or maybe a trip up to the mountains,* she thought. She smiled to herself as she thought of getting everyone going on a Saturday morning. Tim would want to sleep late, and Dan and Mike would turn on cartoons as soon as they got up. *Yes, they would help with a little prodding,* Kathy reminded herself, then felt a deep warmth inside as she thought of each of the children. Tim was maturing so fast. Kathy let her mind drift over the things Tim shared the night before. He had thought about his schooling and conflicts between different areas of his life. But in his conversation, he seemed to know how to look at things in a good way. It was hard to realize this was the same person she watched learning how to walk. There was a lump in her throat as she remembered the time when she would catch him coming down the slide, his eyes wide with excitement.

Her mind started drifting off into sleep again when Dave stirred in bed beside her. Through a half-opened eye, she saw that he was still asleep and on impulse snuggled up close to him. Married 20 years! She could hardly believe it. Sometimes she wasn't sure she really knew this man. He surprised her by his thoughts and reactions, and she could think of her frustration over his preoccupation. But as she drew close, she could feel the deep connectedness between them. She knew his love was deep. The strange circumstance that had them meet each other drifted into her mind. A group of college students happened to go out for a Coke and when they got into the car, Dave was sitting there beside her. She wondered if God had his hand in bringing them together.

Kathy's thoughts turned to God. This past week she had been so busy teaching that God seemed to be pushed into the background. It was hard to keep her mind on him, and feeling a little guilty for not feeling close to him, she started drifting off to sleep again. A few moments later she had a distinct feeling that God was close and woke up to realize that she had been dreaming. But as she pondered the dream, a sense of God's presence seemed to linger. Kathy was struck by the fullness her life had at the moment. There was a richness that she couldn't explain.

Feelings of being blessed turned her thoughts to her son Dan. *He is so much like his father,* Kathy thought. She smiled as she thought of his determination: *Yep, just like his dad.* But then she thought of the way Dan had come up and put his arm around her when she was upset last week. He really had a deep sensitivity. Then her mind drifted to the time he broke out in hives when the boys were left at the grandparents for a couple weeks. He would never say he missed his parents, but you could see his feelings ran deep. She felt a special closeness with Dan.

Her thoughts were interrupted by noise in the kitchen. It would probably be Mike, hungry again. He seemed to be growing like a weed, and food seemed to disappear mysteriously around the house. Then a picture of Mike's excitement over his report card flashed into her mind—how he had to tell her every detail over the phone before she could even get home. She knew he needed her yet and felt a tug in her heart as she pictured his face.

Donna was still half asleep, wondering why the alarm had not gone off. She was about to jump out of bed and wake everyone when she realized it was Saturday. So she settled back in bed, trying to go back to sleep. *Why do I always have to wake up when I could sleep in for once?* Donna complained angrily to herself. She was upset with herself as she tightly closed her eyes, determined to go back to sleep. But her mind started thinking about the weekend. *Boy, this house sure needs cleaning,* she thought, disgusted with the way it had looked the past week. She shuddered as she thought of getting everyone up on a Saturday morning. Jim would want to sleep late, and Derek and Mark would turn on cartoons as soon as they got up. *Yes, they would help clean with a little prodding,* Donna reminded herself, but sighed heavily as she thought of the struggle she would have trying to get them to do their jobs.

Jim would snap back at me immediately, Donna thought and felt anger stirring up in her chest as she thought of the way he would defy her again and again. Jim was maturing so fast and seemed to resent anything she suggested. Donna let her mind go back to the previous evening. Jim had been upset over where he fit in at school, but had blown up and stomped into his room, slamming the door as she had tried to make some suggestions. He turned up his stereo quite loud and did not come out the rest of the evening. The special feeling she had for him when she would catch him coming down their slide now seemed to be gone, and she felt deep heaviness right below her heart.

Donna started drifting off to sleep again when Pete stirred beside her. Through a half-opened eye, she saw that he was still asleep and on impulse turned away from him. *Married 20 years,* she sighed, scarcely able to believe it. She felt so trapped by her marriage. Sometimes she wasn't sure she really knew this man. He surprised her by his thoughts and reactions, and she could think of her frustration over his preoccupation. She could feel the wall between them. She guessed that they still loved each other, but wondered where all the warmth and closeness went. The strange circumstance that had them meet each other came to her mind. A group of college students happened to go out for a Coke and when they got into the car, Pete was sitting there beside her. She wondered now why God had brought them together.

Donna's thoughts turned to God, and she felt a coldness and distance inside. This past week she had been so busy teaching that God was definitely in the background. It was hard to keep her mind on him. She felt guilty for not feeling close, but then started drifting off to sleep again. A few moments later she had the distinct feeling that God was close and woke up to realize that she had been dreaming. She was scared as she thought about the dream, and a deep, unsettled feeling seemed to come over her. Donna was struck by the emptiness of her life at the moment and didn't like that hollow feeling inside.

Her thoughts quickly turned to Derek. *He is so much like his father,* Donna complained to herself. Her mouth went tense as she thought of his stubbornness: *Yep, just like his dad.* She thought of the way he would get moody and not look at her for days at a time. Sure, he had a deep sensitivity, but he sure could punish her and make her feel guilty if she got upset with him. She suddenly felt so controlled by her whole family. She clenched her fists as she felt it was them against her!

Donna's thoughts were interrupted by a noise in the kitchen. It would probably be Mark, hungry again. He seemed to be growing like a weed, and food would disappear mysteriously around the house. She remembered the way he denied eating things and felt a wave of disgust over his sneakiness. How many times had she warned him that she better not catch him in a lie again, but it just seemed to be getting worse. She just couldn't trust him anymore. *He's really going to be in trouble if this continues,* Donna thought as she sighed to herself. The whole family seemed to be falling apart and she didn't feel like holding it together any longer. She was aware of a deep pain inside as she got up to fix coffee.

Having a Good Spirit

And so we have two people, Kathy and Donna. Outwardly, their lives are identical, but inwardly their lives are very different. What is this difference? What is present in the one life but not in the other? The difference that makes Kathy's life so much richer, more meaningful, and worth living than Donna's life is in Kathy's *spirit.*

Having a good spirit is to have an excitement about life and energy for whatever is to be done. A good spirit is to be at peace with self and with others. A good spirit is to be warmed by God's presence. On the other hand, bad moods that seem to linger and linger, deep resentment towards others, and cynicism about life indicate that a person's spirit is in trouble.

Life with a good spirit is worth living. Life without such a spirit becomes heavy and difficult. The externals mean little. A person could be poor, struggling day to day to keep from getting more deeply into debt. A good spirit would make this person's life so much more worth living compared to that of someone who was wealthy but troubled about many things. Thus a person can be sick, dying, deeply in debt, or have some disaster strike and still be in good spirits.

What, then, determines whether one is in good spirits? Externals do not produce one's spirit. The *quality of one's relationships* is what affects the spirit.

But, before we get any deeper into an understanding of what one's spirit is and what affects the spiritual nature of life, how about doing a check on your spirits. Are you in good spirits? Pause for a moment and take the following test.

What Are Your Spirits Like?

For each question check the response that most closely describes you:

1. What are your moods like, and how long do they last?
   - ( ) I am seldom troubled by a bad mood, and when I get upset, I am usually over it in a few hours. (3 points)
   - ( ) I do get into a bad mood from time to time, but it usually is not too bad and does not last more than a day or so. (2 points)
   - ( ) I can get into some pretty bad moods, and sometimes they can last for several days or more. (1 point)
   - ( ) I am plagued with bad moods, and sometimes they last for weeks. (0 points)

2. What is your energy-level and your excitement about what you are doing usually like?
   - ( ) I am usually interested in what I am doing and have a number of things I look forward to doing each day. (3)
   - ( ) I can get involved in things around me, but find myself bored and pressured some of the time. (2)
   - ( ) I often have trouble motivating myself and feel heavy and frustrated with what I am doing much of the time. (1)
   - ( ) I seem to have no energy most of the time and see little, if anything, truly exciting about my life. (0)

3. What is your consciousness usually like—clear and easy-to-focus concentration, or cluttered and unfocused?
   - ( ) I usually feel pretty much together and find it easy to concentrate on what I am doing or what others are saying. (3)
   - ( ) I know my mind wanders some and I have unsettled moments, but in general I can concentrate when I need to. (2)
   - ( ) I catch myself running old things through my mind and often feel somewhat troubled inside. (1)
   - ( ) I almost dread being by myself because so many things that I can't get out of my mind come back to haunt me. (0)

4. What is your fantasy life like?
   - ( ) Many of my creative thoughts come as I let my mind wander, and I value that time to be by myself. (3)

( ) Many of my fantasies are unrealistic, but sometimes I can get a better understanding of myself as I pay attention to my fantasies. (2)

( ) I know I daydream too much, and most of my fantasies are totally unrealistic. (1)

( ) I seem to fantasize most of the time and sometimes get so involved with the fantasy that it begins to seem real. (0)

5. How are your relations with others? Is there good contact and closeness?

( ) I look forward to being with those close to me, feel free and open and in good contact when I am with them. (3)

( ) I can feel close to people, but have trouble sometimes being honest and open with my feelings. (2)

( ) I have some trouble with close feelings and feel myself closing in when a deep conversation starts. I usually keep things light. (1)

( ) I usually don't feel like I belong anywhere and have trouble feeling that people really care about me. (0)

6. In your relations with others, how do you react to frustration?

( ) I can get angry when I'm hurt, but I usually find a way to clear things up and normally can understand the other person's reason for doing what they did. (3)

( ) I have a temper or can get "pouty" easily, but I usually try to clear things up when I get a better hold on myself. (2)

( ) I get upset easily, and it takes a good long time until I feel like talking to that person again. They usually have to make the first move. (1)

( ) My temper or moods seem to control me, and there are times I really don't care when this happens. (0)

7. What is your relationship with yourself like? Do you feel deeply good about yourself?

( ) I normally feel good about myself and have a deep feeling of warmth and rightness inside. (3)

( ) I have good feelings about myself, but tend to feel guilty and upset with myself a good part of the time. (2)

( ) I don't like myself very much and am often upset and down on myself. (1)

( ) I always feel like I am fighting myself, don't trust myself, and often would like to be someone else. (0)

8. How well do you know yourself? Do you have a deep understanding of yourself?
   ( ) I find it quite easy to decide things and will follow through when I commit myself to something. (3)
   ( ) I sometimes agree with people when I don't really feel that way and then regret some of the things I get committed to. (2)
   ( ) I am confused much of the time and afraid of making the wrong decision, so I put things off. (1)
   ( ) I always seem to be fighting myself and feel stupid much of the time. I often put myself down. (0)

9. What is your relationship with God like? Do you trust him?
   ( ) I have a deep feeling of God's presence and feel as if this faith will hold me up no matter what happens. (3)
   ( ) I know God is real, but doubt plagues me when I imagine something bad happening to me or others I love. (2)
   ( ) God seems so distant when things trouble me, and I usually feel only guilt and vague discomfort when I think of him. (1)
   ( ) I am petrified of getting sick or dying, so I don't let myself think of anything past today. I don't feel anything holding me up. (0)

10. Is your life filled with meaning or do you get cynical easily?
   ( ) I am aware of the beauty and mystery of the world and am fascinated by the new ideas and people I encounter. (3)
   ( ) I don't appreciate the things around me all the time, but I can enjoy some of my experiences. (2)
   ( ) I feel suspicious and resentful much of the time and find myself looking for hidden motives and the possibility of being used. (1)
   ( ) It's easy for me to be cynical and to see nothing but bitterness and phoniness around me. (0)

Add up the number of points for the ten items and use the following scale to assess the current state of your spirit:

25 or more points .... You are definitely in good spirits.
20-25 points .... You usually seem to be in decent spirits.
15-20 points .... Your spirits could use lifting up.
10-15 points .... There seem to be some deeper spiritual problems.
Below 10 points .... Your spirit is in trouble.

Don't take your score on this little quiz too seriously. It certainly does not give a perfect measurement of your spiritual life at the moment, but it is designed to get you to thinking about the many things that do go into being in good spirits. What emerges from the quiz is the realization that being in good spirits depends upon the *quality of your relationships.* Your spirits will be good if 1) your relationships with others are characterized by love, openness, closeness, and warmth; 2) your relationship with yourself is honest, with deep, good feelings of self-worth and an appreciation of your abilities; and 3) your relationship with God gives you something to believe in and to direct your view of life and its meaning.

So, if these three basic relationships are healthy, characterized by love, your spirits will be in good shape. Or to put it another way: Spiritual happiness comes by 1) *loving* God with all your heart, soul and mind and, 2) *loving* others as 3) you *love* yourself! But you knew that already, didn't you?

2

What Is Your Spirit?

Do you know what a *spirit* is? Does the term conjure up some vision of a thing that looks like a white sheet with holes for eyes—or of something that goes bump in the night? When you hear the words, *spiritual life,* do you immediately picture sitting passively in church, listening to things we all "should" be doing? Does the term *spirit* have much real meaning to you?

Let's try to give this term some specific meaning. A spirit doesn't have flesh and blood and cannot be detected by our senses. A spirit is nonmaterial and cannot be measured by any physical means. But this does not mean that a spirit does not exist! It is real and is the most important thing present at any given time! A party that has a bad spirit is "the pits," but the same party with a good spirit present is well worth attending. The spirit makes all the difference. A school's spirit is crucial. A college with a good spirit is exciting and alive, but the same college whose spirit has broken down is doomed to struggle to find itself.

The Marriage Spirit

Perhaps the easiest place to begin in our definition of a spirit is in a look at the marriage relationship. In *The Spirit of Your Marriage* I described the spirit as the quality of the marriage relationship at any given moment. Such a spirit is easy to sense. It shows up in the quality of the contact between the two people. If the contact is frequent and natural, with the desire for further contact, then a good spirit is present. Take a look at the good spirit between Tom and Deb:

> Tom and Deb were working around the house on Sunday afternoon. He had been preoccupied with some project but started wondering where Deb was. He took a break and wandered around the house, finding her in the den. He slipped up behind her, startling her as he grabbed her around the waist. She pretended to be petrified. "One of these days, you'll be sorry," she teased, but ended it with a kiss. They chatted for a moment; then Tom went back to his project.

Tom did such a simple thing, but Tom's spontaneity and Deb's playful response indicate a good spirit between them.

So what is that *good spirit* between Tom and Deb? If you would look into the den the moment Tom put his arms around Deb, all you would see is *two persons*. Searching as much as you like, you would still find only the presence of two physical persons. Yet *three* live persons are actually present, and the one you can't see is actually the most important person in the whole situation!

So who are these three persons? Tom and Deb are definitely present, but when they are together something else emerges. This third person comes into being from the merger of the spirits of these two people who are in relationship with each other. This third person is the *spirit* of their relationship.

The spirit or third person represents the whole—the oneness that Tom and Deb have together. This whole is greater than the sum of its parts, because it is made up of the parts (the two persons) *plus* their relationship. And their relationship has a personality of its own.

Think of a marriage that is in bad shape right now. You can talk to the husband alone and find him to be a sensitive caring person. The wife may also be open and pleasant with you. But see them together, and both are changed! The sensitivity and openness change to hardness and tension. The personality of the bad spirit between them dominates their individual personalities.

Are you still having a hard time with this definition of a *spirit?* Certainly trying to picture a third, spiritual person at the point where two lives merge is a bit difficult. Perhaps it would be helpful to picture the spirit as the bonding that holds the marriage or family together. The whole is formed as the relationship deepens and its bond of love and understanding is strengthened. The spirit is like the ligaments of a body, holding the individual parts together in a whole. In a marriage the ligaments are the spiritual qualities of the relationship that bond the two together into one.

That Third Person

What two people feel about each other at any given time is present when they interact with each other. These shared feelings at the interaction point form the personality or spirit of the relationship. Picture yourself in a room with two other people. On your right is someone you really enjoy being with; on your left is a person who upsets you very much. Imagine looking at the person on your right. Don't you actually sense something good between the two of you? Can't you feel the presence of that good spirit? As you look at each other, doesn't something precious pass between the two of you? Couldn't you call what passed between you something of a spiritual nature? Didn't your contact with that person do something to your spirits? You actually feel more alive and in better spirits yourself relating to the person on your right.

Now shift to the person on your left. Something keeps you from wanting to look in that direction. Now, don't you feel something between the two of you? Can't you describe this "something" as a *bad spirit?* Relating to this person certainly affects your spiritual life. As your eyes meet, you feel a coldness pass between the two of you. You feel less alive at the moment, and a heaviness or guardedness replaces your own good spirit. It's hard to be in good spirits when in contact with this person.

So every time you form a relationship with someone, a spirit is present. The two of you are no longer just two separate persons, but you are now a part of a wholeness that this spirit represents. When you are together, you will always have to reckon with the third person that embodies the quality of your relationship. A *bad spirit* makes life with that person miserable, but a *good spirit* makes life well worth living. In both cases the people remain the same; the spirit between them makes the difference!

The spirit is actually a personality independent from the other two persons and has a will of its own. If there is something between my wife Kathy and me, for example, I cannot will it away. I may want to have those good feelings toward her again and even be determined to have a good spirit when I next see her. But as soon as we come into contact, whatever I willed is overcome by the spirit between us at the moment that goes where it wills! The spirit has a will of its own. It cannot be controlled or manipulated by either Kathy or myself. We may pretend or cover up our awareness, but there is a real presence of the spirit between us that won't go away by pretense. Its reality deeply reflects the quality of our relationship at the moment.

So the spirit is not a static thing. The spirit is constantly flowing—like the wind—reflecting the changing quality of our relationship as we share things, hurt each other, confess to each other, come back into contact, and are reconciled to each other. Working on our relationship when Kathy and I are together really means nurturing that precious spirit. This is our spiritual growth together.

The Spirit Within You

Let's now take a look at another place where a spirit exists—within a person. You know you have a spirit. Perhaps you don't know much about that spirit, but you know when you are in good spirits. When your spirit is alive, you have energy and excitement about what you are doing. When your spirit is broken, you feel apathetic, drained, in conflict with yourself. But where is that spirit inside?

Since a spirit exists between two people who are in relationship with each other, *your own spirit exists within the relationship you have with yourself.* In this way, your good spirit would reflect that you feel deeply good about yourself. At the moment you relate well with yourself; you love and trust yourself. So, if you want to find your spirit, look at the intersection point between you and yourself.

You are really two people. You talk to yourself. You get down on yourself for doing something stupid and congratulate yourself for a good accomplishment. You might say to yourself, "Why did you put this off so long?", or "Well, you did it again. You blew your diet last night!" Then you feel guilty.

Who are these two "people" inside you who talk to each other? Current brain research gives us a clue. The *spirit-brain* research indicates that every person really has two somewhat separate consciousnesses inside, represented by the two hemispheres of the cortex of your brain. The two can communicate but seem to remain two separate ways of processing information. In split-brain people (where the corpus callosum has been severed), the right hand actually does not know what the left hand is doing.

There is much more to this research. But for our purposes in looking at the two people inside each of us, let me summarize the two different ways of processing information. If you are right-handed, your left hemisphere probably contains your speech center. The language ability of this "person" inside you allows you to think abstractly—to think about things in a detached fashion. This is the person that thinks back over what you have done and makes value judgments about your actions. This is the "person" inside that says, "Boy, that was really dumb!" Let's call this person your *head*.

Your right (or nondominant) hemisphere does not detach, but looks at things more holistically (pattern-recognition rather than sequential processing, to use the technical terms). This person inside seems to be more expressive of your impulses and feelings. This is the person inside that says, "I'm just not in the mood to study." Let's call this person your *heart*.

So at any given time, both of these "persons" inside are present. As you talk to someone, your *head* is dealing with what is being said and your *heart* is dealing with what you are feeling. If these two conflict, you give a double message. Your *head* may give a good, socially-acceptable, "It's good to see you again," while at the same time the other person inside (your *heart*) will give a nonverbal negative message. Thus, if you don't have a good relationship with yourself, others will find it difficult to relate to you.

When these two persons inside you are in conflict with each other, your energy is blocked. You spend much of your time fighting yourself. Then there is a power struggle going on inside with both sides trying to win and dominate the other. That puts you in *bad spirits*. You are anything but free.

Picture a sailboat on the lake. If the wind is pushing against the direction the boat is headed, the sailboat must tack back and forth with agonizing slowness to get anywhere. But if the wind is pushing in the same direction, the boat glides along with ease.

Now think of the two persons inside you. If they are pushing in opposite directions, most of the energy is used up in the struggle (like "I really should finish this report, but I'm just not in the mood to do it"). But if your head and your heart are pointed in the same direction, things seem to be done with ease.

Let's look at someone whose head and heart are struggling against each other:

Ginger was so frustrated with herself! She was dating a person she really liked, but always seemed to be in conflict when she thought of him. She was so afraid of losing him that she would give in to anything he wanted to do. She hated herself for being so weak and felt used much of the time. But when she thought of being more assertive, the fear of losing him hit again. She would go back and forth in her mind, like a rubber band snapping. Then she would sigh and try to forget about it for a while. Her thoughts never seemed to go anywhere.

Ginger had a spiritual problem. Her relationship with herself was troubled, leaving her in bad spirits most of the time. Her head focused on the way she went against her values by giving in. She was disgusted with herself and constantly put herself down. Her "head" would determine to do things differently the next time she was with him.

But the other person inside (her heart) felt a deep loneliness. If she followed her head she would be alone again and her heart couldn't stand that possibility. Her heart just did not like the way her head always put down her needs and couldn't trust her with control of things. So the two persons inside of Ginger went on fighting each other. This bad relationship with self showed up in her lack of energy and excitement about life. Her spirit was broken.

Your head seems to control your determination to do something. Your heart seems to control your moods. When these two do not relate well together, your determination is sabotaged by moodiness. These two sources of energy collide with each other and stay in conflict. Your energy is blocked, and your spirit is in trouble.

The conversation of a person blocked in such a manner would go like this: "I guess I should do it, but I don't know when I'll get around to it," or, "I really want to, but I'm not sure I should."

When a person has a good spirit, both persons inside are in harmony with each other. Such a person can simply say, "Yes, I *will* do it." To decide on something and follow through with it without undue self-conflict is the basis of true will power

I am reminded at this point of one of Christ's directives: "Let what you say be simply 'Yes' or 'No'; anything more than this comes from evil" (Matt. 5:37).

This decisiveness comes from a good spirit between the two persons inside and not from one person (like your "head") simply overpowering the other. If your head wins the struggle, this can create the appearance of decisiveness (will power), but unfortunately a decisiveness which is on quicksand. Your heart will sabotage your mood and you will have trouble following through: your heart just won't be in what you do.

Your Relationship with God

Up to this point, we have looked at two types of relationships—between two people and within one's self—that determine whether you are in good spirits. But there is yet a third place to look for a spirit.

There is another relationship that we all have that affects our spiritual lives, whether we care to admit it or not. Everyone struggles to find something to believe in—something that would give life meaning. Each personality must have an organizing principle to unify consciousness and give direction to life. This organizing principle must be something that transcends self, otherwise the system will not have direction and purpose. This organizing principle or the person's faith becomes the basis of identity, values, and meaning in life.

For the Christian, the special relationship with God through Jesus Christ is the organizing principle that gives life meaning. And a special spirit lives at the intersection of this relationship! This spirit is the merger of the Christian's spirit with Holy Spirit and creates the quality of the relationship a person has with God. It is a "Special Spirit" because this is the only relationship in which one of the two persons is completely faithful! God's Spirit is constant. God's yearning is for all to be saved—to be in relationship with him as part of the body of Christ. The Holy Spirit, then, is an expression of God's yearning for us—of his constant love toward us.

God's gift of his Spirit draws us into that special relationship. As the Holy Spirit dwells in our hearts, we can truly call God "our Father" and deeply understand that we are his children and heirs with Christ in his salvation. This is our identity and the organizing principle of our lives. Our relationship to him gives meaning to our lives.

Let's look at someone in need of this Spirit:

> Walt had lived long enough to understand people. He had been burned too many times and was not about to trust anyone completely again. In business and in his personal life, he realized it was a good practice to always have a way out. He was shrewd, and no one would have his back to the wall again! He learned well not to take people at their word without double-checking and making sure the legal side was taken care of. He could take care of himself!

Walt was certainly self-sufficient, but a lonely and somewhat pathetic person. He was so afraid of being taken advantage of, forever suspicious of all his interactions. It was as if he were condemned to live in the private hell that his hurt had created for him. He had lost his capacity to trust and to hope. Life could be nothing more than self-protection and suspicion.

When trapped in such a state of mind, we find it easy to spot plenty of evidence to keep the distrust growing. Walt's capacity to get out of the trap himself was severely limited, if not impossible. He was in a vicious cycle. His mistrust would breed cautious reactions from others, which in turn fueled the mistrust. Walt desperately needed something powerful to break out of this cycle—something that would once again give him the capacity to trust and hope.

The Holy Spirit is the power that can restore Walt's faith. With his spirit broken by hurt and mistrust and his energy turned in on himself, Walt needs a source for a new spirit! In his weakness, his relationship with God can give strength.

This may sound like pious talk and good-sounding theology. The realness of the Spirit, however, makes those words powerful. The Holy Spirit is a real person with power, searching out our hearts. When we cry, "Abba, Father," we are expressing that merger between us and God—where his Spirit and our spirit meet. The special spirit dwells at that intersection point in our relationship with God and is as real as the spirit of our other relationships.

Through the Holy Spirit, no matter what your spirits may be like at the moment, your life can be turned around. Even if depressed or rejected, you can be in good spirits again. If you feel a deep sense of guilt and are not able to forgive yourself, you can be in good spirits again. That's our hope and our faith. Our Father made this possible through our Lord, Jesus Christ. What a comfort! What good news!

3

Your Soul Yearns
for a Right Spirit

Now, where does the energy for your spirits come from? For a spirit to form in your relationships, there must be something within you that needs, searches out, and is fulfilled by the relationship that is subsequently formed. Perhaps this potential to form a spirit originates in your *soul*.

Inquiry into the nature of your soul brings up the purpose of God's creation. What is your intended role as part of his world? Why are you here? What is it that will make your life full and happy? If your life is only a random occurrence, then life is only what you can make of it. But if you were created for a purpose, then surely there is a blueprint embedded within you that would direct this purpose. This embedded blueprint is your soul.

Your soul carries the potential for you to develop good spirits in your life. Embedded in your soul is your capacity to love and develop relationships. Since God is love, your soul reflects the image of God. Your capacity to love and the good spirits that can be formed out of that love are an image of God, for we were created in his image.

Thus, your soul represents that deep yearning for love. And it is this *yearning* (like all of creation groaning, yearning for redemption) that is at the root of all other emotions. Time and time again I have gotten down to this deep yearning in my counseling. Let's take a look at Jim:

> Jim sat there defiant. He had been in trouble and was referred to me for counseling. He felt he had to come and just stared at me with hard lines around his lips. He first appeared apathetic with, "Well, I guess I'm stuck here for an hour with you." Then as I struggled to listen and get into his world, the apathy seemed to turn into bitterness: "Sure, you say you're concerned. Just take away your fee and then let's see how concerned you are about helping me." When I searched deeper, the bitterness gave way to anger. "Who says I have to stay here and be hassled by your stupid remarks?" Still more searching and Jim started sensing my concern, so the anger moved to a deeper emotion—hurt. "No one really cares for me, I've had to watch out for myself all my life." Then fairly quickly after that came the deepest emotion that surfaced for just a moment in a wistful look on Jim's face and the hint of shakiness in his voice: "Yep, no one really cared about me."

Jim, like everyone, was basically struggling to find something out of life. He was very unhappy. Deep down there was still that yearning for someone to care, but this yearning was covered over by his hurt. He had never felt cared for or affirmed. That yearning was still a spark of life in his soul. Jim could still be touched; that potential, although covered over, was still there.

Our awareness of this deep yearning usually comes when some part of the yearning is not satisfied. We yearn for relationship with others, with our self and with God. These are, perhaps, the three deepest needs of any person which, if satisfied, make life a rich, fulfilling experience, but if not satisfied, make life a painful, unfulfilled search for happiness and purpose.

Yearning for Relationship with Others

Every person needs deep relationships. The feeling of not belonging anywhere or that no one really cares is a devastating feeling. Without the deep, rich emotional interaction with others who deeply care about you, your emotional life is constricted and pushed into fantasy for expression. There is a hellish quality to life without such deep relationships:

> Jerry is a self-assured man who always appears confident and in control of his life. He had been married, but said that such a life-style was not for him and was divorced in a few years. He owns his condominium, makes good money, and is free to date around, take a weekend for golf, or anything he might choose. You can always find him at singles parties, ready for a good time. But there is a forced quality to his good times—almost an obsession to find something exciting to do. He has experienced about everything, but there is a hollow ring to his life. Gradually he began to lose interest in things and was plagued with bouts of depression. He would wake up in the middle of the night, even after a heavy dose of sleeping pills, with a deep, empty feeling. He knew that he could die tomorrow and no one would be deeply affected. He has lots of friends, but no one would really care that deeply. He just cannot get rid of that nagging emptiness.

Without someone to care for and without the feeling that others deeply love us, we feel an inevitable deep emptiness inside. The yearning for closeness and intimacy cannot be filled with anything except love. One of the most pathetic and heartrending experiences of my life was visiting a nursing home to find a completely depressed woman staring into space all day, wishing she could die. She had children and relatives, but all caring had long since been destroyed in her relationship with them. No one had come to see her for over five years. No one cared if she lived or died. Her loneliness was indescribable. In a word, her spirit was dead.

Such deep yearning for relationships with others is the basis for much of a person's emotional life. I know that my moods are basically affected by my interaction with Kathy and my three sons. I am definitely in good spirits when we are close, but can get moody, easily upset, or depressed when something is wrong with these four special relationships. My deep relationships represent the basis for my emotional life. If there is a good spirit in those relationships, my emotions are stable and life is exciting and fulfilling.

Yearning for Relationship with Self

You have to live with yourself every moment of the day. As much as you may try, you can't get away from self. So if you have a bad relationship with self, life is a constant struggle and endless conflict. The yearning for a good, deep relationship with self is really a yearning for peace. There is a hellish quality to life without that deep inner feeling of peace. Barbara yearned for that peace:

> Barbara had blamed all of her problems first on her parents, then on her boss at work, then on her roommate, and now on her husband. She lived with a constant, "If only," as she thought, "If only I could get a new job," or, "If only he would change." But as I looked deeper, it was evident that Barbara did not like herself at all. She was constantly going on a diet, trying to quit smoking, determining to start a strict exercise program, and angry at the amount of TV she watched. Her first thoughts in the morning were how she wasted her time the previous day. Then she would think over all the stupid blunders she made and wish she would have kept her mouth shut. She would think of hundreds of things she should do, but then find herself daydreaming and getting nothing done again. She was so disgusted with herself and seemed to stay edgy and angry. She was hard to live with. Barbara was not at peace with herself.

Without that good relationship with self and without the deep feeling of peace inside, life becomes an inevitable conflict. A person's energy system is locked in the struggle with self, and there is little energy available to reach out to others. Instead of one's energy being aligned so that the two persons inside are working together, the two persons are in conflict. The energy goes nowhere, and the spirit inside that person is in trouble.

For such a person, there is a deep yearning for inner peace. The soul is deeply troubled, giving the person no rest. The conflict seems to be ever present, and the person's life is hellish. Without the deep, good feelings about self and with an almost total lack of self-esteem, there can be little spirit for life. As I look into such a person's eyes (windows to the soul), there is no spark of life or playful search for energizing contact, but only a worried, troubled gaze.

Yearning for Relationship with God

Everyone needs something to believe in—something outside self that gives meaning to life. "My soul longs for the Lord" is a theme that echoes throughout the Psalms. This yearning or thirsting for God comes from a deep recognition of the human condition. A person's awareness must be based on assumptions about reality that come from outside the person (revelation). Without an external starting point, one's consciousness is doomed to endless questioning and to a deep recognition of its capacity to rationalize. Without this definite starting point, consciousness turns in on itself.

To put it another way: to search for the meaning of life from within one's own life is an endless circle of rationalizations. And the person is further plagued with the realization that his sights are nothing but self-justification. Betty was trapped in this endless circle:

Betty had her life in order. She had a good career, had developed some good friendships, and had worked hard, and finally had what she considered financial security. She had settled back to enjoy life and felt content about all she had accomplished. But then a conflict developed at work, and her job suddenly was in jeopardy. A long court battle over her rights in keeping the job began to drain her finances, and in her constant worry over the situation her health began to deteriorate. What she had worked so hard to build suddenly began to crumble. She mustered up more of her famous determination to continue to fight. She had nowhere else to turn. She was the only person she believed in and trusted. She was trapped in her faith.

Without that good relationship with God and without the deep feeling that he is real and present in our lives, life is a terrifying struggle. Instead of the freedom this relationship with God gives to experience life, death raises its ever-present head. Anxiety over sickness, economic collapse, job disintegration, and being used by others infuses one's consciousness with worry. Life carries the sentence of deep anxiety and struggle to gain more and more security. And when one's self-made system—one's *identity*—begins to break down, the demonic forces of apathy and cynicism begin to take over.

The yearning of the soul for something to believe in is real. It can be covered over and ignored for a while. But obsession with keeping one's body fit or with surrounding one's life with evidence of security betrays the deep weakness inside. It is the yearning for someone to be there when things fall apart. It is the yearning for a heavenly Father who can give hope when there is no hope. It is the need for a wellspring that keeps one's energy from hitting bottom. It is the need for faith.

The Key of Love

A person's soul and its deep yearning that pervades all of a person's life is thus the potential within each of us for being in good spirits. The soul is the purpose of God's creation locked up within each person. Like the analogy of a lock and a key, it is there to be unlocked so that our lives may be fulfilled. So if the right key is turned in this lock, a good spirit is the result. This is the heart of "righteousness" in our lives.

God's law shows the proper way to put things together. Since our souls reflect his will or the purpose of his creation, he gave us the law for our understanding of what would make our lives full and happy.

It is always easy to see the law as a set of directives from above, as a cruel taskmaster, as something we'd better follow or else. Instead, God loved us so that he couldn't stand to see us floundering without direction and doomed to hell, both on earth and in the after-life. God, in his mercy, gave us the statement of his purpose (his will) to give our lives direction once again. And so it was with much affection that the Israelites looked upon the *torah* (the law). It was a deep sign of God's loving kindness to them—something they could trust since it came from the Author of Life! His law shows how things should fit together for our lives.

And we know how to achieve such good spirits. The key that unlocks our souls is love—the deepest affirmation that we can have. Love can take a hard, cynical person and transform her into a sensitive, caring individual. Love is the key to God's creation—for God, himself, is love. Once again, Christ has summarized for us the way to spiritual happiness in his summary of the law. "You shall love the Lord, your God, with all your heart and with all your soul and with all your mind; and you shall love your neighbor as yourself." If love characterizes these three critical relationships in our lives, we will be in good spirits. Love is the bonding element of a good relationship with others, with self, and with God. The potential is there for all of us in our soul:

Laura had never been affirmed. She was not really wanted as a child and remembered the constant phrase, "Things would have been so much easier without you." Her father paid little attention, and try as she might, she didn't seem to do anything he was proud of. She tried so hard to please him, only to be ignored and put down time after time. Her mother had problems of her own, and in the time they spent together, her mother seemed always to be suspicious of what she had done and constantly accused her of different things. She longed for an end to her miserable life and stayed alive out of sheer determination. She never remembered being warm and happy inside—never cuddled by her mother or secure on her father's lap. So Laura was searching—trying to please but never feeling as if she belonged anywhere. She was puzzled over life and wasn't sure what her search was all about.

The potential was still there for Laura, but nothing had touched her soul. She so desperately needed to be loved, but lost hope that there would ever be love. Though she looked so self-sufficient, in many ways she was desperate. She appeared so hard on the outside, yet there was such a deep longing on the inside for someone to break through.

And how do you know what your soul is yearning for? Since there is a "right" way to put things together, you instinctively know when things are not right. Your soul is like a deep voice inside that speaks out. It is as if God's law were written in our hearts—embedded in our souls. When any of the three critical relationships do not have the proper fit, your soul is troubled. The deep, inner voice will begin to trouble the person's sleep. This is the classical understanding of your conscience and how it works.

You may try to drug this voice with sleeping pills, alcohol, or by working 16 hours a day, but the voice remains. Something is deeply troubled about your life and you know it:

Max had all the reason in the world to separate. His wife had been unfaithful, and he had endured so much pain and criticism in his relationship with her. So he decided it was his turn to be happy. He moved out and determined to find some real happiness for a change. He started with bars and picking up whomever was available. He prided himself with his new reputation and constantly "preached" the relief and happiness single life had given him. But strangely, after some months, he found himself driving by his wife's house, wondering what she was doing. He would find excuses to call her and would get mad at himself for doing so. He even started dreaming about her, and one day when he happened to see her with another man, he lost control, became insanely jealous, and threatened to kill the man. Frightened with his own behavior, Max went back to his apartment and took another look at his life. It was as if "he came to his senses." He knew at that moment that he really did love his wife and was just kidding himself with his other affairs. He resolved at that moment to work on his marriage, even if it meant going for counseling. He now was ready, for he knew what he wanted.

And so our soul is God's gift to us—it is his image within us that gives us the potential for life at its fullest with good spirits. When this potential is unlocked through our relationships with others, with self, or with God, a good spirit is the result. A good spirit means energy and excitement about life. It means love, joy, peace and all the other qualities that make life worth living. God meant for us to be happy, and all his creation reflects the goodness of this intention.

PART TWO
SPIRITUAL PROBLEMS THAT WEAKEN A GOOD SPIRIT

In this section the reality of sin and evil stands out. What God intended for us is so often destroyed. The destructive forces within us that produce broken spirits are the focus of Chapter 4. Bad spirits, the demonic, and Satan are the subject of Chapters 5 and 6.

4

A Broken Spirit Is Natural

If life was meant to be such a good experience, why am I discouraged, even depressed, so often? Where is my good spirit? Where does it go at times? Where is the warmth, closeness, and oneness between people? Marriage too often seems to be a battle. The closer the spouses get, the more they seem to hurt each other. Just how many marriages are happy, anyway?

And where is inner peace? What can take away those troubled thoughts and disquieting feelings? Why can't I sleep well at night? Why can't I just turn things off?

And where is God when we need him? The world seems to be going to hell, and all we have are some promises he made to another age. Why didn't he heal my mother? She was such a good person, why did she have to die? Just what has God done for us lately? He surely doesn't seem to remember that he created me. I just seem to be adrift. It's hard to see much of a purpose in all this—sickness, death, poverty, war, hostages, violence, cruelty. Where is God when we need him? When I ask this question over and over, all I hear is silence.

Do children set out to destroy their lives? Does a person

enter marriage with the intention of working toward a divorce? No one chooses to be miserable and unhappy. So where does the unhappiness come from? Could there be the force of sin and evil in the world that seeks to destroy our good spirits?

You and Others

Breaking the spirit of a marriage, family, or friendship seems to happen naturally. Two people in a close relationship inevitably hurt one another. Feelings get hurt, intentionally and through misunderstanding. These hurt feelings tend to collect in the center of the relationship (at the intersection point, where the spirit lives). If these hurt feelings do not get expressed, they turn into "hard feelings." In turn, those hard feelings start building a wall between the two people.

When you are hurt, the first thing you do is to break contact with the person who hurt you. You may look away, or stomp out of the room. Then, if these hurt feelings between the two of you linger on, you don't feel like looking at the other person. In fact you avoid direct eye, voice, or touch contact.

Then a vicious cycle occurs. When you get hurt, you break contact. Breaking contact puts you into a bad mood, which further keeps you out of contact. A bad mood is nothing more than being stuck with emotions that have nowhere to go. Once you are in a bad mood, the most natural thing is *not* to seek to restore contact. Instead you tend to hurt back in some way. But as you get even, the other person also has to get even. Then *you* have to get even again, and the cold war goes on and on, allowing the feelings to harden.

So what begins to destroy the spirit of any relationship is not so much the hurt feelings themselves, but the way the hurt feelings are allowed to collect at the intersection point of the relationship and gradually develop into hardened feelings. And as this wall of hard feelings grows higher and higher, the relationship loses more and more of its contact. Greater chances for moodiness occur as the spirit breaks down more and more.

When there is a good spirit between two people, there is

little chance for misunderstanding, and thus much less chance for the two people to hurt each other. But when the good spirit starts breaking down, what is said is no longer taken "in the right spirit" but is easily taken as a put-down. Further hurt and brokenness is the result.

And the deeper the relationship, the greater the potential for the two people to hurt each other. The more emotion invested in a relationship, the more the yearning of the soul is fulfilled. But the more emotion invested, the more powerful the mood created when the energy is blocked:

> Donna and Larry met at a fraternity party at college. They had both been around quite a bit and weren't interested in a really serious relationship. So they started spending some time together and were happy picking at each other. When they would get on each other's nerves, they would stop seeing each other for awhile. They argued and would step out on each other, but it didn't seem to bother either of them since they looked upon the relationship as more of a convenience than anything else. Then after some months had gone by, something started happening to Donna and Larry. They didn't seem to have much fun anymore and much of their time was spent arguing and criticizing. The good spirit had broken down and they couldn't seem to get along with each other—but they couldn't seem to just walk away from each other either. It seems that they had gotten involved with each other without acknowledging it and now had the capacity to hurt each other more deeply—creating the moodiness and defensiveness.

These bad moods that result from hard feelings between two persons may have some connection with our sinfulness. To sin is to go against God's will. Since God's will is for us to love one another, sin is the breaking down of love in these relationships.

Because of the grip sin has on our lives, it is not possible to keep from breaking the spirit of any relationship. If you doubt this, just try to do something positive in your relationship with your child when there has been complaining and whining all day long. The resentment inevitably builds up until you *don't want to* be kind to that child. Just try to be patient when you feel the child is being manipulative. Or what about your spouse or close friend? Just try to keep a good spirit going when you have been criticized for several hours straight—or when you have been ignored for several days. Your mood has shifted. At that moment *you don't want to* restore the relationship. You want to hurt back by lashing back or sulking in the corner. And that is all too natural and powerful.

Your Relationship with Yourself

Breaking the spirit of a person with self is all too easy to do. You can break children's spirits by turning them against themselves. Let's look at a conflict created inside of Tommy:

Tommy wanted so much to please his father. He wanted to be looked on as a big boy, so he was excited when his dad asked him to help with some painting. He just knew he could do the best job ever and his father would be so proud of him. He was in such good spirits, eager to help. A few minutes later, dad came to see how he was doing, and immediately reacted, "Why did I ever think you could help me? I should have known better. You're no help at all. You just make more work for me. Now get out and let me try to straighten out what you messed up." Tommy left with head hanging and spirit broken.

Tommy wanted so much to please his father, but he ended up feeling incompetent and worthless. He was turned against himself, and all the good energy that came from his spirit was now blocked. He just wasn't good enough to please his father, so he thought, "Why try anymore?" Yet he still wanted to make his father proud of him. Don't you feel the conflict inside Tommy at that moment? What else could he do but return to his room, and sit and stare with his mind blank and his energy listless?

It is also easy for you to break your own spirit. The precious relationship you have with yourself is broken when you do something that goes against yourself. There are two ways of going against yourself. Remember that the two persons inside you have different needs and functions. Your "head" thinks about what you want to be, sets your goals, and evaluates your actions. It contains your value system. So one way to destroy the relationship with that person inside is to do something that would go against your values, as Paula did:

> Paula had always dreamed of a happy married life and had decided to stay a virgin until she married, believing that she would have so much more to bring to the marriage if she would "save herself." But then she met Brian. He seemed to be the perfect person for her, and she felt more and more tempted to give in to his gentle persuasions. One night they had gone out for a special dinner, had shared a bottle of wine, and she felt especially close to Brian. Before she knew it, they were alone together, caressing each other. She had a fleeting thought that she should stop, but the mood was right and she gave herself to him. It seemed so right at the moment. Paula awoke from a nightmare in the middle of the night and then remembered with horror what she had done. It no longer seemed right, and she started crying. Suddenly she did not feel the same for Brian and the nauseating thought came that he had now gotten what he had been after. She got up and took a bath, feeling dirty and ashamed. Something was so different inside her. The good, warm feeling about herself was gone, and she hated herself.

Paula went against something she valued highly. She did it willingly and woke up to the realization of what she had done. Such a violation of what she had so strongly believed in was enough to turn her against herself. It was enough to break her spirit.

The second way to break your spirit has to do with the other person inside. Your "heart" is more related to your feelings and emotions. If you do not value your needs and feelings, but go against them and put them down, you also hurt your relationship with yourself. Jeff did this:

> Jeff always took responsibility for everything. He would immediately see whatever needed to be done as his job, and

when things didn't go right, he blamed himself. He felt guilty much of the time and put himself down. He seldom paid attention to his own needs, and thought it wrong to let others know what he felt and needed. Jeff gradually became more and more depressed. He seemed to lose most of his energy for life. It seemed that his spirit was broken.

When a bad relationship develops inside, you lose trust in yourself. Much of your conversation with yourself becomes negative and nonproductive. Starting things and not following through, wavering back and forth about something, and wanting to sit and stare off in space are evidences of a broken spirit. Neither person inside likes the other. The end result is a poor self-image, moodiness, depression, and a lack of excitement about life. One's energy system is blocked.

Take a moment and listen to the conversation inside your head. Is there good discussion, leading to a clear feeling of direction, determination, and will? Or is there endless confusion and conflict? Which of the two conversations below would be more typical of what goes on inside your head?

HEART: I'm not feeling so good.

HEAD: Well, we need to work in the yard or do some fixing around the house.

HEART: I feel like sitting down and reading right now —I'm tired of rushing around.

HEAD: Well, the yard and house have to be taken care of some time. When would be a good time to do it?

HEART: I need some time to relax and enjoy myself right now. How about in an hour?

BOTH: Okay, let's delay for a while and then tackle the yard and house.

HEART: I'm not feeling so good.

HEAD: The yard is a mess and the house needs a lot of work—you've been letting it go again.

HEART: But I'm tired and don't feel like it.

HEAD: There you go again—lazy and trying to get out of work.

HEART: If you say so. *(Begins to walk around the yard, depressed, looking at what there is to do.)*

HEAD: Boy, you sure let things pile up.

HEART: Aw, there is too much to do. I don't know where to start.

HEAD: Well, let's do something. *(The person stands there, staring at the work.)*

The first conversation goes somewhere. There is a conflict over what "should" be done and what you "want to" do. The conflict is talked over and is resolved with good energy. In the second conversation the same conflict is evident. But in this conversation there are put-downs that create guilt feelings. The conversation goes nowhere. The "head" notices all that should be done, yet the "heart" is not in the mood to do it. With no energy to get on with it, the person just stands there lifeless, locked in internal conflict. Whatever the "head" decides, the "heart" is not in it! The person's spirit is in trouble.

As the relationship inside further deteriorates, a person begins to feel nothing but hardness, pain, and ugliness inside. When all trust of self leaves, everything becomes a horrendous pile of conflicts, as it did for Pam:

Pam never remembered any affection when she was growing up. She fantasized a lot about closeness and tenderness, but her life was virtually void of such feelings. So when Doug started talking to her at work one day, she felt hope for the first time. He was separated and found Pam easy to talk to. He told her of his struggles, and she listened. A few weeks later they went out and he shared more deeply with her, and for the first time she experienced real affection. That unlocked something in her, and she wanted to be with Doug more and more. He was at first amused at the way she worshiped him, but then gradually started getting tired of her constant attention. He started demanding more and more from her. He took money, favors, and then started being more open with his disgust of her. She got more desperate and clung more tightly to him, doing everything he wanted—even though some of the things were degrading. He would talk more and more nasty to her and treated her like a dog, but she still clung to him. Finally, when he flaunted other women in front of her, she couldn't take it any longer. She broke off from him, but she could no longer trust herself. For the next three years, she would not even look at a man. She punished herself endlessly by remembering all the degrading things she allowed herself to be put through. "Oh, you were so stupid!" she would remind herself again and again. With such obsessive thoughts and without hope of getting her need for closeness satisfied, Pam settled into a deep depressive state. Her spirit was destroyed.

Going against one's values and failing to deeply understand one's needs and one's humanness break down the relationship inside. Things not being right inside reflect a broken spirit. Without this feeling of rightness inside, persons begin to doubt their integrity, self-worth, and morality. As a result, the person then gives off double messages and resorts to playing games with others. Intimacy and the capacity to relate to others are deeply affected.

A broken spirit within a person reflects sinfulness in our lives. Coveting is an example of this. To covet is to put yourself down by comparing self with others. As you covet another person's success, for example, you fail to appreciate your own value as one of God's children. To go against one's deep values (which is really God's law in one's heart) is likewise an example of sinfulness.

You and God

Breaking the Spirit between you and God is all so easy and natural. The Holy Spirit is eager to build a dwelling place in your heart—creating an identity around which your life and consciousness can be constructed. Nevertheless, anything that would stand in the way of such an identity breaks down that spirit. For when we allow other things to become more important than the Holy Spirit, the Spirit's work in our life is blocked. This blockage begins to destroy that spirit in our lives.

It is easy to find *things* to identify with, things that appear to be the road to fulfillment. There are many things that have the misguided power to energize us and tap into our religious yearning. Everyone wants to be somebody—to have significance that is more important and lasting than the temporary influence of the present. So many things reach out with the promise of giving more to life—the promise of some kind of immortality. Diane was searching for something greater:

> Diane never considered herself very important. She was shuffled around as a child from foster home to grandparents to aunts and uncles. When she finally earned a scholarship to college, she was determined to make something of herself. She found a natural talent for drama and started spending more and more time around the playmakers of the college. By her senior year, the theater was all-consuming, and she dreamed of breaking into something big. She went to New York after college and with a few connections, landed a few parts the first year there. She wrapped herself completely around these parts and the promise of more to come. All else seemed forgotten in her quest for that big part.

Drama had consumed Diane's yearning. Drama had tapped into her religious sentiment, and she sank all her energy into its promise of giving meaning to her life. But as she became more famous, strangely enough she did not feel any happier inside. What she dreamed would be so fulfilling let her down. Her success just did not bring that deep inner happiness. Her zest for life started eroding. She began to get cynical. She blamed the theater and its phoniness for her emptiness inside. She did not understand that this yearning was to fulfill God's purpose.

So it is that many things sidetrack our religious yearning. Fame in football, tennis, theater, business, writing—the list is endless. All give the promise of identity—of something that can give life a fullness and meaning beyond the basic insignificance of self. But all these sources of identity can break down. There are always others waiting to snatch one's "fame" away.

There is one identity that will not sidetrack you, your identity as a child of God. This identity as an heir with Jesus Christ to eternal life is not something that anyone can take away. The yearning of one's soul for meaning and immortality is really a yearning for a relationship with God. And when this yearning is fulfilled, we know deeply that God loves us and calls us his own. The Holy Spirit builds a temple in our hearts which grows and grows as our relationship with God deepens. This identity with Christ given by the Holy Spirit is a wellspring for our lives. Such an identity gives our lives energy that never ceases and holds us up through sickness, death, and whatever else might crash into our lives.

So when this spirit is broken in our lives, it becomes the ultimate loss. The foundation of our identity and thus of our whole consciousness is lost. Rather than having the wellspring of God's eternal love, we are then left to our own accomplishments for the source of meaning in our lives. That means we take ourselves too seriously, and once we do that, we're in trouble.

With our spirit broken, we turn in on ourselves. Turning in on ourselves, we center our identity on our accomplishments or good fortune. Being forced to center one's identity on some personal accomplishment or lucky break is frightening. This identity has to be carefully guarded and protected. To protect it, we turn in on ourselves, and our lives become selfish. We are no longer free to take risks and let ourselves become vulnerable in our other relationships. We are no longer free to love.

5

A Bad Spirit Enters

At 16, Ed was vulnerable. His broken spirit left his yearning completely unfulfilled. His energy was blocked, leaving everything churning inside. There was a deep yearning inside for peace, and the thought of dying was one of his more pleasant thoughts. His broken spirit left him so vulnerable. He desperately needed something to feel good about. That is when he discovered a good feeling. After Ed had minor surgery, his doctor prescribed strong medication with a narcotic base. That was all Ed needed to discover a new feeling inside. A different sense of well-being warmed him a few minutes after that first pill, and he had a good feeling about himself for the next several hours. His head felt different—peaceful and good for a change; gone was that ever-present anxiety. He took two pills the next time. Soon he was taking the pills regularly.

A bad spirit is a false way of giving a person energy—a false way of tapping the yearning of the soul. In Ed's case, the potential for feeling good about self and about life was tapped by a narcotic. It set him free, free from his anxiety and free from the horrible ugliness inside. For the moment it gave him a sense of happiness and a good spirit. After two pills, life seemed more worth living.

The bad spirit is not the chemical, but the *hope* that such a drug gives. It is the promise of a better life—of a good spirit. Moreover, a bad spirit offers this promise persuasively, making it seem so innocent. It's hard to argue against feeling good, while you are feeling good.

Let's use Ed's good feeling with narcotics as a way of conceptualizing how a bad spirit operates. Such a spirit gets its energy from the same place a good spirit does—from the yearning for closeness, peace, and meaning that comes from one's soul. A bad spirit also develops a relationship that taps that energy. It has the capacity for producing good feelings and energy for one's life. But it is not a *right* spirit and comes from a *false* fit—a relationship with destructive elements. A bad spirit initially causes good feelings and frees up one's energy, but will eventually lead to greater destruction.

Since Ed's bad spirit was related to narcotics, let us use the opiate receptors of the brain as an analog to the development of good and of bad spirits. The body produces its own narcotic, enkephalyn, that unlocks these opiate receptors. This is the "right" key, and the unlocking of these receptors produces feelings of well-being.

Narcotics produced outside the body also have the power to unlock these receptors. In Ed's case, the narcotic in his pain medication unlocked these opiate receptors. He felt good. He wanted more. The drug could do what his own broken spirit could not do—give him a better feeling inside.

Why call this apparent good feeling a *bad* spirit? It is a bad spirit because it ends up producing more brokenness! A person seeking to be in good spirits by taking such a drug pays a price for these "good spirits." Once the key to unlocking the opiate receptors comes from outside the person, the body ceases production of enkephalyn. The person becomes dependent upon the outside source to unlock the opiate receptors and loses his or her freedom. They now need the drug, and it is now in control of their life.

Once Ed accepted this way of feeling good about himself, he gave up his freedom. More and more of the drug was now required to produce the same good feeling. It seems to be a basic rule of brain chemistry that externally-derived chemicals gradually lose their potency, requiring more and more of the chemical to produce the same effect. That is part of the nightmare of getting hooked.

What happens when the person fails to pay the price of being hooked? Since the body has ceased production of the internal opiate, failure to take more of the narcotic after four to six hours leaves the body completely without the ability to unlock the potential of the opiate receptors. The result is pure hell! The anxiety that begins to develop is indescribable.

> Ed was desperate! He was taking up to 14 percodin (narcotic pain medication) a day, and he was out of pills! His usual source just informed him that he couldn't get any more and Ed was coming apart inside. He was ready to do anything to get his hands on those precious pills. As the day wore on, he stopped caring about anything else. His whole consciousness was intent upon getting another fix. He was a desperate, pathetic 16-year-old. He was crying, begging, pleading—anything for that good feeling again. That's when he was introduced to an injection of heroin. The good feeling was back tenfold. Ah, this was worth any price!

The original good feeling that Ed found in the pain medication had turned on him. His life was now driven by a powerful force. His craving for the narcotic was demonic. He was possessed by his craving. He had lost his freedom.

The body's natural production of narcotic is the *right* fit for the opiate receptors. The right fit is the only way to unlock the receptors without paying a price for doing so.

Let's look at bad spirits in the broader context of one's life. Remember that a bad spirit is a false way of tapping one's energy. It is a false way of putting things together, bypassing the right key (the key of love) to produce the "spirit." The false "fit" initially causes energy and good feelings and gives the illusion of freedom. Often a bad spirit so closely resembles a good spirit with its right fit that the false fit goes unnoticed at first. But once a person has sold his soul to such a spirit, its true nature emerges. The bad spirit becomes demonic and begins to haunt the person. Gone now is even that illusion of freedom, and this last state of the person is far worse than the first. The result is more brokenness and destruction.

Bad Spirits Arising from Brokenness Between Two People

Jane was hurting. Bob seemed no longer to have much interest in her. She knew she was hard to live with some of the time and did not like herself when she remembered the ways she had attacked him the past year. But his almost complete lack of interest in her was hard to take. She had many fears in the back of her mind. So when a friend suggested that he might be stepping out on her, she was ready to suspect that. Suddenly his behavior made sense. "So that's what has been going on," she thought to herself. She started snooping through his billfold, checking up on his activities, and following him at times. She was determined to catch him. She just knew she was right about his affair.

The stage was set for Jane. There was a broken spirit in their marriage, and much of their communication had broken down. Jane was hurting and searching for the cause of the brokenness. She had many painful thoughts about her own behavior and was feeling guilt inside. She was vulnerable to a bad spirit. And it came to her. When she heard about the possible affair, her consciousness fit it all together, and she actually felt much better. "So it was his fault all along," Jane concluded. She could feel energy again. Instead of feeling empty and lifeless, Jane was now filled with new energy. She spent hours of "exciting" time checking on Bob. She no longer felt the need to sleep much of the time. She had a focus for her broken spirit. She was a determined woman.

But her energy came from a bad spirit! Even though it gave her more energy and picked up her spirits, it did not leave her feeling deeply good inside. Instead, there was a growing sickness the more she checked up on Bob. Her feeling of brokenness and hurt began to turn into hatred. She had trouble looking at him, thinking only of his deceit and his affair. She became obsessed with her search, going back over anything he would say for some clue. In a sense, she now had a demon. She was driven by energy that had turned on her. She had lost her freedom and could see nothing else but his deceit.

The interesting point here is that whether or not Bob was having an affair did not make much difference to Jane's demon. In this case he really was not going out on her, but was feeling the weight of her accusations more and more. Thus he began to have less and less desire to be with her. But even if he were having an affair, Jane had accepted that rationale to get her energy back again. Her search led to more brokenness between the two of them. She was trying to feel right inside at the expense of the relationship. Driven by her hatred and suspicion, she ended up with a demon.

Demons use a person's own energy that has been turned back on self. They arise from that deep yearning that has been hurt —energy that has been blocked. This energy becomes misdirected from the original yearning by a bad spirit. It now turns on the person, coming back to haunt. The person becomes driven by this new impersonal force.

Bad Spirits Arising Out of Brokenness Within a Person

Tommy had loving parents, but he felt they were too strict. He was afraid to ask them if he could ride his bike to a friend's house. He knew they would say no. So he told them he was just going to ride around the neighborhood. He then slipped over to his friend's house, but someone saw him. His parents asked where he had been and he said vaguely, "Oh, just riding around." As they tried to pin him down further, he denied going anywhere and finally blew up at them for never trusting him. He slammed the door with indignation. He acted as if he were unjustly accused. Then he set out to prove that he had not gone over to the friend. He immediately called his friend and asked him to lie. He called the person who saw him go over there a liar—even got into a fight with him. Tommy became obsessed with proving he didn't do it. He had a demon. He had lied, and now the lie had come back to haunt him. He got in deeper and deeper.

A good spirit carries with it a good, deep feeling of peace within self. Doing something to destroy that spirit leaves energy stirred up inside. It is not hard to discover when one's inner peace is broken. Tommy's lie initially gave him more energy. He avoided punishment and didn't have to face what he had done. But the bad spirit turned his energy back on himself. He was now possessed with proving himself right.

When a person's spirit is broken, it is convenient to find a way to feel better about self. But the very way to feeling better about self can become demonic. The easy lie that Tommy came up with gradually consumed more and more of his thought. He lost his freedom.

The bad spirit takes the energy (yearning to feel deeply good about self) and gives a temporary good feeling by a false fit. This *false* fit does initially bring relief by being rationalized as a good or right fit, but eventually leads to greater brokenness. A person can go against principles and rationalize by saying, "Everyone else does it." However, such self-righteousness is thin and has to have a constant expenditure of energy to keep up the feeling of rightness. The apparent good feeling about self has to be defended and constantly proven. A truly good spirit and the freedom it gives is not present.

Bad Spirits Arising from a Broken Faith

Cynicism is demonic! The faith of a child is free and open. Faith arises from one's yearning for something to believe in. The Christian faith is the expression of a good relationship with God.

But when that relationship is broken, when it seems as if God has let us down, when dreams for our life have been shattered, then we are vulnerable to a bad spirit. It becomes tempting at this moment to get our spirit back by idealizing—by building our own fantasy world and putting our hope in that world. This is just what Barbara did:

> Barbara was disillusioned. She had tried to make her marriage a good one—everything her parents' marriage wasn't. She had thrown herself into pleasing her husband, but he turned out to be a different person than she thought he was. His initial tenderness and attention gradually turned into harshness and distance. Deeply hurt by his numerous affairs, Barbara finally sought divorce. Soon after, she met the person of her dreams. He was all she ever hoped for—tender, attentive, and so good to her. She dreamed of the life they would have together. He was just perfect!

Barbara had gotten her spirit back—but at quite an expense! She idealized the new man she met and made him her source of happiness. She idealized him into her "god" and worshiped him, wrapping all her hopes and dreams around that relationship.

So you can imagine what happened when her new husband turned out to be human. Barbara tried to hold on to her idealization as long as possible and strongly denied any hint that he was not all she made him out to be.

Joan also ended up idealizing someone, but for a different reason:

> Joan remembers her anxiety hitting when she stood there, watching in horror as her precious baby gasped for breath in the hospital. She realized the child might not make it. All of her dreams for her daughter were shattered. A feeling of dread had come over her. "What if she dies . . . ?" The half-thought struggled to reach her consciousness, but it was too shattering to think about. The child recovered, but the anxiety remained, like a feeling hovering in the back of her mind. It was ever-present, like something she couldn't push away—a blackness that seemed to get larger and larger.

Joan's anxiety was related to the way she had idealized her only child. All of her dreams were wrapped around her little baby—her dreams of closeness and fulfillment. She couldn't take the thought of losing her, so the anxiety guarded against such a thought. But as she initially felt better by blocking out the possibility of losing her baby, the anxiety started demanding more and more of her energy. It had become demonic, driving her consciousness as she desperately tried to hold to her idealization and dream.

So, what is driving your consciousness right now? If you have the same disturbing thought, morning after morning, you may have a bad spirit. You may have your own "demons" that disturb your sleep. What are they?

6

Where Do Bad Spirits
Come From?

But where do these bad spirits come from? At the moment of brokenness in a person's life, there are countless offers for instant healing and quick roads to feeling good again. These promises of a good spirit are tempting, for they bypass the more slow, painful route to rebuilding relationships.

There are three sources of bad spirits, one for each of the three different relationships that can produce the good spirits in our lives. Bad spirits are produced by *self-justification, rationalization,* and *idealization.* In contrast, a good spirit is produced by love.

Self-justification

To make ourselves feel better about a broken relationship with *another person,* we turn to *self-justification.* There is something powerful in being able to justify one's actions. The need to struggle with the brokenness is over. A false peace is established—and a bad spirit emerges. Look at this bad spirit in Borg's case:

Borg and Sandy came to see me. Borg was a little more reluctant than she was. However, both were definitely willing to try to save their marriage even though he had moved out. They had come three times, and it looked as if things were going to turn around. A better spirit was developing between them, and he was thinking about moving back home. But the fourth week Borg called and curtly announced he was not coming back. Within the next week he had filed for separation.

What had happened? One day the marriage looked so promising, but the next day it was hopeless. Only later did I find out what had caused the drastic shift in Borg's attitude. It happened like this:

Borg was debating about going back home—he really wanted to, but was afraid he would be trapped just as he was before. It felt so good to be out from under the daily struggle. But the sessions had definitely made a difference—if only he could trust that Sandy would continue trying after he moved back. So with those thoughts troubling him, he went out with a friend to have a few beers. His friend wanted to help him— to give him the best advice. So when he opened up about his dilemma, his friend, without any bad intention, gave him the justification he needed to go ahead with the separation. His friend simply said: "Borg, you'd be a fool to go back to her. I know how she is. She'll never forget that you left her. She'll make you pay for it the rest of your life."

That struck a deep chord within Borg's perception. He had some of the same fears and mistrust of Sandy, but to hear his friend say them so clearly and forcefully put things together for him. It made good sense for him to go ahead with the separation. He couldn't live the rest of his life constantly reminded of his faults. Now he had all the justification he needed to quit trying.

So that's what a bad spirit is! Borg felt good and confident when he called me. His voice had decisiveness and strength in it. He was no longer broken and uncertain. He could now justify getting away from the broken relationship. But in the long run he was not all that happy. He still had some deep feelings for Sandy, and his bad spirit ended up coming back to haunt him. Let's see how long Borg's decisiveness lasted:

> Sandy was crushed by Borg's decision to finalize the separation and sought counseling. She was able to acknowledge her hurt and once again get in touch with her yearning for closeness. It was almost a year later when she met another man. She dated him casually at first, hesitant about another relationship at that time. But then Borg found out she was dating. He started following her and started calling, threatening her if she went out with him again. One night he was waiting at her door when the other man brought her home. He was insane with jealousy.

So Borg ended up with a demon! His initial good feelings over justifying his separation did not last. His deep feelings for Sandy were still there, and the justification turned into jealousy when he had to face Sandy's affection toward another man. He was a driven man!

So where do the easy justifications come from? There is a force of evil in this world that is at work destroying the potential God gave us for good spirits. The justifications that so easily pop into our minds or that so easily spill out of the lips of well-intentioned friends do have a source. That source is ultimately Satan himself!

The devil is still alive and at work among us today. He supplies a culture at any given age with ample self-justification to produce bad spirits out of the brokenness. He comes to rescue with the easy way out. How many of these have you used on yourself or as well-meaning advice to others?

"Well, you can't trust him anyway."
"He doesn't really care."
"They won't miss it."
"You've done everything you could."
"He got into the wrong crowd."
"I don't really see how you can stand that constant nagging anyway."

"There are other fish in the sea."
"What he doesn't know won't hurt him."

It is no accident that the word Satan means "to split apart"
or "to divide." It is God's will that we love—that we have a
good spirit with him, with others, and with ourselves. Satan
works against that purpose. He seeks to destroy those good
spirits. He does this initially by making his path seem to be a
good one. Satan is cunning and subtle. His bad spirits always
seem good and reasonable at first. In fact, Satan's path so
often resembles a good spirit that we can tell the difference
only after the true nature of the spirit has emerged.

And no one is needed to teach you how to justify your actions. "He did it first," seems to be the unlearned response of
a child accused of fighting. Self-justification just "pops" into
our minds. "But he, desiring *to justify* himself, said to Jesus,
'And who is my neighbor?'" (Luke 10:29).

Rationalization

To make us feel better about a broken relationship with
ourselves, we turn to *rationalization.* To be able to explain
away our dubious actions is to rationalize. Martha was good
at rationalizing:

> Martha was sitting in my office, angry at her brother. They
> just had a blowup and he accused her of spreading the family
> gossip around. She admitted to me that she did talk to some
> friends, "But," she continued, "after all, I needed someone to
> talk to. Besides," she continued, "I did not mean for it to get
> back to him."

See how much of our conversation is laced with rationalizations? They make us feel better. They take away the possible
blame we would have to face without them. How many of
these have you used?

"I couldn't help it."
"But I didn't mean to."

"It wasn't my fault."
"How could I know?"
"It was just an accident."
"Everyone else does it."
"One more won't hurt."
"I deserve this."
"I'll worry about it later."
"What's wrong with it?"

Our rationalizations make us feel better by keeping us from facing the brokenness inside. They soothe our broken spirit. But the energy they give us is a false fit and produces a bad spirit. Something deep inside knows we are being dishonest. So each rationalization puts us one step further from a deep sense of honesty and peace inside. It just does not fit. It doesn't tap into the very source of our energy. So it takes more and more energy to keep up the rationalizing until we end up with a demon. Jimmy tried this path:

> Jimmy tried to tell himself that it wasn't all that important anyway. *So what if I didn't make the baseball team,* Jimmy thought. He didn't really want to spend all that time practicing. He didn't really care. But Jimmy started getting depressed, and thoughts about playing baseball would flash through his mind. He got to where he couldn't even watch a baseball game on TV. He went from loving the game to never mentioning it.

Jimmy did not acknowledge his hurt. Rather the easy rationalizations popped into his head, and he felt better with his "sour grapes" attitude. But something didn't fit deep down. His energy turned into depression.

Idealization

To make us feel better about the *negative aspects* of our lives, we turn to *idealization*. Idealizations pop into our heads, and we buy the hope they give us. But these are bad spirits because the initial good feeling they give eventually shows its true nature. Then disillusionment sets in.

> Paul was very upset. He shook his head as he said, "I don't know why I ever trusted my son! I thought when I put him to work for me, things would straighten out with him. Here I did everything I could, but then he steals from the business. I'll never trust him again!"

Paul had put all his hopes of straightening out his son by putting his son to work for him. He now was totally disillusioned and cynical about his son ever amounting to anything. Paul had set himself up for the end result; his idealization set the stage for his final cynicism. He had felt good about his son coming to work and put unrealistic hopes on that situation. It would have been an "easy" way to solve the family problems. But the problems went much deeper and the bad spirit could then show its true nature. Paul's cynicism was demonic. He had had it with his son.

But don't you idealize? Haven't you thought:

"If only he would do that."
"When she finishes, then . . . "
"Just wait until I get out of school."
"Next time will be better."
"It won't happen again."
"It'll blow over."
"Time will heal things."
"There's always tomorrow."
"I'll take it one day at a time."
"When I finish this book."
"I'll have more time next week."

These idealizations may be bad spirits in disguise, authored by Satan. He makes us feel better. He soothes the brokenness of our faith.

So who is this Satan? I know he is more than I can tackle. He can turn my energy against itself in ways past my knowing. His power resides in getting us to accept an easy rationalization or substituting self-justification for the pain of facing our brokenness. He knows that our capacity to rationalize is infinite.

The power of Satan lies in getting us to "sell our soul" to him to ease our pain. Buying into one of his justifications, rationalizations, or idealizations gives him access to our souls. Satan then has control of our energy system, and he can use it to further destroy our relationships. His end is destruction. His temptations are subtle. It feels so good to blame the other person for the broken marriage. It is soothing to rationalize one more drink. It is energizing to idealize an easy solution. But none of these ways is the *right* way. They are all shallow. Yet the power of these bad spirits is compelling. And they are ever-present to offer their quick pathway to being in good spirits again!

PART THREE
HOW YOU CAN BE
IN GOOD SPIRITS AGAIN

What can you do about your spiritual life? How can you be in good spirits again and maintain these good spirits?

The first principle expressed in the following chapters is to discern which spirit is present. There are three types of spirits that need to be recognized: *bad spirits, broken spirits* and *good spirits*.

The second principle lies in the proper use of law and gospel. When a *bad spirit* is present, it is proper to use the law as a call to honesty in order to break the person's comfortable rationalization. If, however, the spirit is a *broken* one, forgiveness and the reconciling power of the gospel are needed. For the broken spirit, the gospel renews, and this renewal is the basis for being in good spirits again. And when there is a *good spirit*, this energy needs direction. Thus the law as direction from a loving Father is needed for a good spirit to continue.

Using the gospel for a bad spirit is like "casting pearls before swine." Using the law for a broken spirit will only discourage and dishearten. And the confrontive use of the law for a good spirit will only produce unnecessary burden, resentment, and guilt.

The third principle is the deep awareness that a good spirit is part of a good relationship. Your spiritual life is really an expression of your relationships with God, with others, and with yourself.

7

The Holy Spirit Is Powerful

The Holy Spirit is the spirit of the relationship between the
other two persons in the Godhead. The Holy Spirit proceeds
from the Father and the Son. It is a *Holy* Spirit because the
relationship between the Father and the Son is one of perfect
love. Out of this loving relationship, a third person proceeds,
the Holy Spirit.

The Holy Spirit is sent to each of us out of God's deep love
for us—a yearning for us to be his own. God's Spirit seeks to
be the basis of our identity—to dwell within our hearts so that
we can become a temple of the Holy Spirit. When God becomes our Father, we experience relationship with him. There
is a spirit of that relationship—a special spirit created by the
Holy Spirit!

The Power of the Spirit

The Holy Spirit is powerful. Yet his power lies not in forcing
us to obey God, but in convincing us of the truth. He does not
coerce us into believing, but works toward developing our
faith. The Holy Spirit centers our lives, tapping our yearning

for something to believe in. In that way, he produces energy. In the book of Acts, whenever the Holy Spirit fills any of the apostles, the next words are usually, "and with boldness he began to speak." By faith, the Holy Spirit gives us the boldness and power of our convictions. The Holy Spirit provides a basis for our integrity, a wellspring of strength in our lives.

The dwelling of the Holy Spirit in my heart gives a grounding for my life. There is energy when all else seems to fall apart, hope when things look hopeless, boldness and energy to speak my convictions. There is always a source of renewal of my broken spirits.

As the Holy Spirit dwells in the temple of my body, I will always have energy to begin anew. He constantly renews my relationship with God. The Holy Spirit is a drawing force—a yearning, a pulling from God himself. Since I am known by God, the Spirit gives me a basis for worth. I can form my identity around that worth, for I am a child of God. There is boldness in that conviction, a basis for energy in such faith. The Spirit centers my life around God and renews my spirits. Through him, I can be in good spirits again, no matter what mess and shambles I have made of my spirit. God's love is that strong. It had to be when I received the following message:

> The words hit me like a bombshell. "Mom died last night," I heard brother Ted say in a shaky voice in Reutlingen, Germany. We had just returned with our students from East Germany, and he caught us in Mainz at the youth hostel. A deep sadness began at my stomach and lodged in my throat as I echoed the words to Kathy and our boys. The quick trip back to Indiana was like a dream, but when I stood over her casket, the reality was piercing. She was dead! There are tears in my eyes yet as I write this. She loved all of us so. But at that moment something else happened to me—something I also still feel strongly. It is a feeling of calm and peace beneath the hurt and sadness. As I looked at her so still and lifeless, it was like *a friend* speaking to me from somewhere deep inside, "Your mother's love is still with you, Dave. You will always be warmed by her as you remember her closeness to you." The sadness was still there, but a deep comfort seemed to rest beneath it. I felt in good spirits, even at one of

the most painful moments of my life. My friend, the Holy Spirit, comforted me.

I would love this deep feeling of peace more often, but I cannot command it to come. The Spirit moves where it wills. That voice came from within me, and I could rationalize it away. I could explain that it was a projection of my need at the moment. I could even analyze the voice as a hysterical illusion brought about by the trauma of my mother's death.

But I won't! As a psychologist, I know about projections and hysteria. But I also know a deeper source of reality. That voice wasn't just my own inner conversation; it was a Friend who came into my life to comfort me. The feeling of peace was too deep for me to be comforting myself. That peace I still have when I think of Mom. It is a good spirit amidst the sadness and yearning for her.

I don't hear that voice often, but I know he is present. Most of the time there are no words, just the constant awareness that there is a depth to my consciousness—that I have a center somewhere, even though I might be far from that center. Sometimes I know the Holy Spirit through a gentle pulling together of my thoughts to God in prayer. Sometimes it's a harsh jolt, reminding me that things just aren't right inside. When I drift away, the Holy Spirit draws me back to that relationship with God.

When my life is shaken up, the Spirit sighs for me more deeply than words can express. He knows me so well. And his understanding—the feeling of being deeply known by God in that relationship with him—touches my spirit. And so I know that no matter what, I can always be in good spirits again. That is my hope. That is my faith.

The Spirit at Work

Let's take a look at how the Holy Spirit touches our lives. He works within our relationship with God and lives at the intersection of that relationship. The Spirit works in us as God communicates with us. He works through the means of grace—the Word and sacraments which are the tools God uses to communicate with us.

God's Word is the proper fit—the right key for the yearning of our soul. God created us, and he knows what we need. He knows what the yearning of our soul is all about. He knows what fits our yearning for something to believe in. Through His Word, we know the truth, and the truth sets us and our energy free. The truth centers us and lets us live at our deepest level—the depth of our convictions. With boldness we can live, with all personal integrity and character, with direction for our lives. The Holy Spirit gives that boldness of conviction and renews a right spirit within us—a spirit of that right relationship with God. The Spirit makes us whole.

The power of the Holy Spirit is opposed to the power of Satan. Satan takes the depth out of our lives, destroying our ability for deep relationships, sentencing us to shallowness and banality—life without good spirits. He would have us cynical, bitter, resentful, distrusting, and insulated—a hellish existence with no life at all. He does this by offering what seems to be an easy way to a good spirit—a way that bypasses the *right* way. He would have us feel centered and full of energy with an evil spirit—with rationalizations, justifications, and idealizations.

But it hurts to take a deep look at the truth and see the brokenness in our soul. We would rather keep it covered up and explain away our sin. That's much less risky.

But something deep inside knows the truth. And it is to that deep voice inside that the Holy Spirit speaks. His power is the sword of truth. No matter how drugged our souls may be from rationalizing, drinking, tranquilizing, or explaining away our troubles, that voice is still there to trouble our sleep. Andy heard that voice:

> Andy had control of his life. He finally broke away from his troubled background, had written his parents and brother out of his life and moved away. He was relieved and happy—free to begin anew. He didn't want any responsibility or involve-

ment as he made new friends quickly. He was making good
money and doing anything he wanted to do. He was happy.
Or at least he thought he was happy. After a year and a half
of making all the singles parties, going on skiing trips and to
the beach, and having weekends all to himself, he began to
have trouble sleeping. He got medication to help him sleep,
but even in his drugged state, a certain restlessness wouldn't
quiet down. Something just wasn't right with his life, and
deep down he knew it! His soul was troubled.

So Andy came to see me—not really knowing why he had
come, but sensing something was deeply troubled inside. His
life seemed to lack depth and vitality. There were no commit-
ments and little desire to be committed—only an emptiness
that nothing seemed to fill. He really had little to live for. He
was tired of the singles games and a little too dependent on
alcohol. He was tired of trying to get up for a good time. It
was a struggle to have fun. He seemed dead inside, drained
of all his energy. He had no center, no basic, deep source of
energy to tap. He had little to believe in, and he knew it. He
was through trying to kid himself. He was ready for a change.
He was ready to dig in and become honest about his life.

It is to this voice—to this yearning—that the Holy Spirit
reaches. God wants us to believe in him—to be one of his own.
He is the fulfillment of that yearning so deep inside. The power
of God's Spirit is the truth that deeply fits our lives. And this
Spirit of God is not afraid to confront the destruction in our
lives.

The source of the power is external; it comes from outside
ourselves. The power is the truth of God's Word, combined
with God's caring. His Spirit conveys this power to us.

His work is nothing you can directly feel. It's not just an
emotion or an enthusiasm. It's not like God sticking a direct
pipeline of energy into your life. The work of the Holy Spirit
is something that deeply fits in your life—a wholeness that is
convincing. He gives you something substantial and true to
identify with. Something deep inside knows it fits. God's love
makes the connection and creates new life within.

The Spirit of Honesty

But there is still another way the Holy Spirit works in your life. He can bring you to faith when you are listening to that troubled voice within, but what happens when you are not listening? What happens when you have drugged that voice or rationalized it away?

The Holy Spirit also has the power to name and to stir up the bad spirits within you. Whenever he confronts the bad spirit, he always starts off with a call to honesty. He begins by asking, "Who are you?" He asks the troubling question, "Are you really happy with your life?"

By what means does the Spirit call us to honesty? He uses the Word of God both as written in Scripture and as communicated to us by fellow Christians. This may take the form of a harsh word spoken by someone who cares about us. Or it may take the form of an observation by a friend—something that just won't go away even though initially denied.

This Word comes from the law—the statement of what is right and wrong given by God, himself. And that Word is troubling: it will stir up the bad spirit and reawaken the deep voice within. It is a call to truth.

And so the power of the Holy Spirit comes from the law and the gospel. The word of truth about what God knows to be good for our lives—the law—cuts through our rationalization. It destroys our self-justification. It calls into question our idealization. It is a call to honesty in our lives.

The other expression of God's love—the gospel—gives us hope. It shows the reconciling power of God's love in Jesus Christ. So our broken spirits can be healed; we can be whole once more. The power of the Holy Spirit reconciles us and renews our relationships. That's the basis for a right spirit.

8

Working on That Good Spirit

Are you in good spirits right now? Just how is your spiritual life? I know what it would take for you to be in good spirits again. You have the potential for it—down deep in your soul. At the deepest part of your person you yearn for closeness—to be loved and to make a difference in someone's life. Loneliness means that this yearning is not being fulfilled. You yearn to feel deeply good about yourself. Depression and anxiety mean that this yearning is not being fulfilled. And you yearn to have something to believe in. There is nothing quite like being excited about and committed to what you are doing. Boredom and that feeling of insignificance mean that this yearning is not being fulfilled.

So to be in good spirits again is to have the yearning of your soul fulfilled in those three, all-important relationships—with God, with self, and with others. To be in good spirits means that you love God with all your heart, soul and mind, and that you love others as you love yourself. And that is the basic message that the Author of us all gives us as he reveals his blueprint for our lives.

Two Directives

In a practical sense, this revelation gives us two good directives for our lives. One is that when the spirit is present within those relationships, it is time to put your energy into working on the relationships. Yet, it is so tempting when things are going well to take these relationships for granted, only to wake up with the communication suddenly blocked and the spirit in trouble.

The second directive concerns what to do when the good spirit is not present. At that point it is tempting to soothe the broken spirit by the ever-present bad spirit, using rationalization or justification or idealization. What to do with the broken or bad spirits will be taken up in the next two chapters.

Let's take a closer look at the first directive—when the relationship is good and a good spirit is present. This is when you have the energy and desire to put into the relationship. Remember the spirit of the relationship is, after all, the wellspring of energy that is present when the yearning of your soul has been tapped. The energy never runs out when the yearning is in the process of being fulfilled within a good relationship. Love never, ever, runs out!

But you need to know how to work on these relationships. What is it that will deepen things between the two persons? Just where should this energy be put?

Use the energy of the good spirit to establish better contact and a deeper understanding between the two persons. When things are good, it is tempting to seek personal happiness (which is the spirit of our age). So, to get your values straight at this point, know where the good spirit comes from. When you understand that a good spirit is a result of deep and meaningful contact, then direct your energy toward such contact in your relationship.

Basically, better contact means to be in touch with self and to be open to others and God. It means working on keeping the channels of communication open, developing skills helpful in relationship-building.

The following are suggestions for skills you can work on. As you read through these, check any that would be difficult for you, ones that you need to work on. Then make a list of these for yourself and review it each day to see what progress you are making.

Relationship Skills: Working on That Good Spirit

ENCODING SKILLS: WORKING ON THE RELATIONSHIP WITH SELF

In this section the assumption is made that there are really two "persons" inside: the verbal self ("head") and the nonverbal self ("heart"). These skills are pointed toward getting to know these two "persons" better and thus developing a better relationship (a better spirit) inside.

Getting to Know Your Nonverbal Self ("heart")

_____ 1. Realize that this "person" inside you relates emotionally to concrete situations. Focus on specific situations as the basis for emotional meaning. Get in touch with the emotion aroused and consciously name the emotion.
I felt sadness when I heard of a friend's death.

_____ 2. Realize each emotion has a physical location in your body. Pinpoint its physical location. Describe its physical characteristics.
My sadness is like a tightness in my throat.

_____ 3. Realize each feeling carries with it an impulse value. Pinpoint what the nonverbal self would really like to do or to say at that moment.
When I feel that sadness, I want to hide my face in my hands and say to myself, "I need a chance to mourn for my mother."

_____ 4. Translate the nonverbal feeling into a verbal analogy.
When I focus on my sadness, a picture of my mother caring for her son pops into my mind, and I realize a deep warmth below that sadness over her death.

_____ 5. Pause for a moment to understand the history of that feeling. Focus on the feeling and remember a time when you felt that same way before.

I remember the same feeling of sadness when the college I served before was closed, and the good spirit of that community had to break up.

_____ 6. Then remember that the feelings of this nonverbal self are valid and worth understanding—that they are not to be denied, put down, or glossed over, but appreciated and integrated into your whole person.

That experience of sadness makes me feel more human and connected.

Getting to Know Your Verbal Self ("head")

Even though you usually are more aware of the verbal self because your consciousness has a verbal base to it, there is an aspect of this self that you can get to know and appreciate more. The key to the organization of this self is your value system, which needs constant clarification and updating as your life changes. Your basic beliefs usually do not change, but new thoughts and experiences need to be integrated with your basic evaluation of life.

_____ 1. Utilize values-clarification techniques. Be aware of what turns you off and what turns you on in other people. Integrate these perceptions with your belief about life. Make sure your values are consistent.

I admire a person who is open to the needs of others and responds to them. This value is consistent with my Christian faith.

_____ 2. Own your values. Make sure you are not just mirroring the values transmitted to you by others. Check to make sure you actually believe in and own for yourself your moral standards.

"Look at Jim, just going around, buttering up people, saying what they want to hear." This is a negative evaluation of Jim's social activity, but do you actually believe this statement, or do you say it because you are jealous of Jim's popularity?

_____ 3. Realize the importance of your value-system. Take it seriously, and don't end up rebelling against it without trying to understand that person inside of you.

"I know I'll be sorry, but I'm tired of not having any fun." This statement suggests a point of rebellion against one's values.

Working on the Integration of the Two Selves

A third force—almost like a third self—needs to emerge inside you to work on the integration of the two selves. Both selves need to feel that they are being taken seriously and that their individual concerns are valid and are being taken into consideration. So write down on a sheet of paper what each self wants to say about a given situation or decision. Then let this "third force" (which is your spirit) work on integrating, neither going against your beliefs nor putting down your emotions. True integration can emerge only from the process of putting both selves in creative tension, working within the intention (good spirit) of integrating instead of having one side or the other win. ("I really shouldn't, but . . ." means that the nonverbal self won at the expense of one's values. Struggling for reconciliation between the two selves would go something like, "I would like to do it, and I am struggling with whether or not I should.") Such a search for reconciliation takes time and is an ongoing process. And this is where the energy of the good spirit can be directed.

CONTACTING SKILLS: WORKING ON THE GOOD RELATIONSHIP WITH OTHERS

Letting Others Get to Know You Better

_____ 1. Start conversations and bring up subjects important to you. Bring your thoughts to the forefront of your brain, reducing the insulation between your thoughts and speech (lowered self-consciousness). Break the habit of letting others set the topic of conversation. Value your own thoughts and feelings enough to risk expressing them.

Since I usually let Kathy start our conversations, this is a skill that I continue to work on and will probably keep working on it for the rest of my life so that I will gradually share more and more of myself to her.

_____ 2. Get emotion into your expression. Break the habit of being guarded as you talk. Let your voice show excitement, anger, etc. and be more expressive in your facial and body movements. Use more "I" words—more self-assertive sentences.

"Well, I thought about saying something, but I'm not sure it's all that important," can be changed to "Hey, I want to tell you something." Command attention.

_____ 3. Learn to assert self without becoming aggressive. Say what you want or what you are thinking, leaving other people the option of responding if they want to. Keep from being manipulative by intimidating other persons or making them feel guilty. Genuinely leave them the option of expressing their feelings. Assert with sensitivity to the situation.

"We never go anywhere anymore," expresses your wish to go out, but makes the other person feel guilty in the process and thus is a manipulative statement. An assertive statement could be, "I would like to go somewhere tonight. I'm feeling somewhat trapped in this house lately." Now the opportunity for the other person to respond to your wish is there without the "aggressive" component.

Getting to Know Others Better

_____ 1. Get into the other person's world and make sure you understand what that person means before you react. See that person's world as different from your own. Realize that you will not automatically understand what that person is saying. Develop an openness to other ways of looking at situations.

I have found that a person who is emotionally expressive usually has trouble understanding someone who has difficulty expressing feelings. It is easy to feel that the person is deliberately hiding something. The reverse is also true.

_____ 2. Actively search for meaning in the other person's world. Follow that person's emotion without feeling you have to do something with the feelings expressed. Let the feelings belong to that person and allow that person to have feelings. Let that person know you understand.

"I'm feeling depressed today," doesn't mean you need to try to cheer the person up with, "Oh, come on, it isn't that bad." Rather you can search to understand that feeling with, "Tell me more."

_____ 3. Control your own reactions until you are sure you understand. Keep the noise-level down in your own head so you can concentrate on what the other person is saying. Keep from becoming defensive about what is being said. Keep from immediately advising, solving, questioning, minimizing, denying, or judging.

"Why should you feel that way?" is a reaction that cuts the other person off. "What's that feeling like?" is more the search for understanding that helps build the relationship.

CONFRONTATION SKILLS: DEEPENING THE RELATIONSHIP WITH SELF AND OTHERS

Keeping the Channels of Communication Open

_____ 1. Develop a habit of daily contact with self and significant others. Share things of relatively minor importance to keep the channel open. Have a place where significant conversation can take place—a place away from T.V. and other distractions. Develop a mood of openness associated with that place, perhaps at a certain time.

Grow to expect significant conversation after supper over a cup of tea; then the spirit will be right when something difficult needs to be confronted.

_____ 2. Learn how to shift the mood of the situation. Work at bringing the conversation from *"out there"* to *"in here"* and then to *"down here,"* so that things of personal, emotional significance can be discussed.

"John is trying to take all the credit for what I've done" is an "out there" statement. Bringing it "in" and "down" would take, "I was hurt today by John's attempt

to take credit for what I had done. I just feel discouraged about my efforts there at work."

_____ 3. Stay with the topic to allow a deeper level to be expressed. Keep your mind from wandering. Sustain good eye contact. Keep from jumping to conclusions and give up impressions or conclusions that do not check out. Let everything get expressed. Admit not understanding and ask for more information.

"Well, I guess that's OK," usually means that more needs to be expressed because it really is not completely OK.

_____ 4. Keep a good flow of conversation going. If the discussion becomes one-sided, reverse the flow of energy. Do not let the flow go in one direction. If you usually find yourself talking and trying to convince the other person, shift to listening. If you usually let the other person set the mood, shift to talking.

It is helpful to be aware of the direction of the flow of energy at any given moment. To do so, consider your eyes as they look at another person. If you are trying to read the other person's face, you can feel the energy coming in your direction. If you are trying to make the other person understand or to feel something, the energy is flowing away from you. With practice, you can learn how to flip that "switch" behind your eyes to reverse the flow of energy.

Raising the Unspoken Issue . . .

_____ 1. Be aware when something is not "right" before it gets too big to handle. Value that little voice that is trying to get through and tell you that something's wrong. Struggle to surface those things in the back of your mind, realizing the value of expressing the unspoken. Risk such expression.

Stop right now and see if you cannot find that "little voice" right now. What is it trying to say to you?

_____ 2. Take responsibility for what is surfaced. Use your own feelings as the issue is surfaced. Keep finger pointed at self when making the confrontation. Give the other person the genuine option of responding or not responding.

*"There's something wrong with you, isn't there?"
raises the issue with your finger pointed at the other
person. "I'm feeling uncertain about what's happening
between us. Can we talk about it?" raises the issue with
the finger pointed at self.*

_____ 3. Confront with the intention of helping, resolving, and
reconciling. Recognize your own intention before raising
the unspoken issue. Do not raise the issue when you are
quite angry and upset, when it just erupts out of you.
Raise the issue in the right spirit.

*"Oh, I've had it! This is the last straw!" Such ways
of raising the issue almost guarantee that the spirit will
not be right and more bad feelings will result from the
confrontation.*

_____ 4. Respond to the issue raised by the other person. Allow full
expression of the sensitive subject. See the importance of
the issue to the other person and trust that person's judgment in bringing it up. Then struggle to fully open up the
issue so that all feelings can be expressed, rather than
diffusing things.

*"I have no idea what you're talking about" diffuses
what the other person is trying to confront.*

FAITH-ENHANCING SKILLS: WORKING ON
THE RELATIONSHIP WITH GOD

Remember that these directives apply only when there is a
good spirit already present through the work of the Holy
Spirit. These directives are part of the ability of the Christian
to *respond* within the relationship the Spirit creates with God.

_____ 1. Make sure there is daily contact with God, not the rote
kind that is nothing but habit, but the personal, direct
prayer Jesus made possible. Prayer and meditation provide such focused contact with God. With such contact,
be aware of the Spirit dwelling in your heart and of the
wellspring of hope and security this relationship gives.

_____ 2. Work at a deeper understanding of God. Get to know his
will more and more through his revealed Word. See Scripture as a witness that all of life is related to the spiritual
and that the creator and preserver of your spirits is God.

Search the Scriptures with the attitude that the Author of us all cared enough to reveal what it takes for our lives to be fulfilled. Use it as a check against your values.

_____ 3. Work toward integrating your Christian faith into your whole perception of life. See the wonder and awe in all of creation. Marvel at the renewal of a spirit and rejoice at the beauty of a good relationship. Be alive in the Spirit!

_____ 4. Then share this perception with others. Witness to your aliveness and hope. Share your growth with your family, as in family devotions. Share with others in worship, seeing it as an opportunity for growth in faith.

_____ 5. See a crisis as an opportunity to be aware of your own limits and your need for God's help and love. Allow your crisis to be a time to experience God's love in the caring of others. Allow the problems of others to be an opportunity to show God's love in you.

Look back over the items you checked and choose the two items that you need most work on. Put a double star in front of these. Then choose other items that you need to put some energy into and put a single star in front of these. Write these in your own words and put them where you will look at them many times a day. Then, when the spirit is willing, put some energy into working on them. Also keep the other items you checked in mind and go over them from time to time so that the energy from your good spirits will be used to deepen your relationships.

The above directives are real and important, but apply only when there is a good spirit present to give the motivation for implementation. If there is not a good spirit present, these items will only be the source of heaviness and guilt as you find it a struggle to get up the energy to do something about them.

In this connection consider the word *responsibility*. The previous items are your Christian responsibility. But if you do not have the energy, if you are without a "good spirit" to motivate you, you cannot respond to them. So your "responsibility" relies upon your "ability to respond." A good spirit is what gives you the ability to respond in a loving fashion—and if a good spirit is not present, you really do not have the ability to respond. Your response will then be tainted with guilt, resentment, and a heavy feeling of "have to." A good spirit gives you the "want to" that flows with desire. "I really should work on this," becomes, with a good spirit, "Hey, can I help you?" *It is in that spirit that the above directives are given!*

9

Healing a Broken Spirit—

Reconciliation

So your spirits have been trampled on and you're depressed and feeling low. Your energy system is blocked. There is nothing to get excited about. You don't really know what's wrong. You just feel down. Something's got a hold of you, and you are irritable, satisfied with nothing, hard to live with.

At that moment you are at a critical point. You are vulnerable for a bad spirit to move in and make you feel energy again. You may feel yourself looking for an affair—for something to stir up some excitement in you again. You may feel yourself looking for something to become angry about—some cause that you can latch onto or some person to talk about and cut down. Or you may feel like pouring yourself a couple of drinks or taking a few pills that will change your mood. Having a broken spirit makes you vulnerable to finding an easy way to put things back together again—a way that will lead to more brokenness, hence a bad spirit.

But, to be in good spirits again, the brokenness must be reconciled. It cannot be minimized, rationalized, smoothed over, drugged out, or short-circuited by anger. The brokenness must be dealt with in an attitude of need and honesty.

Finding the Blockage

So you first need to find the blockage. Where and why did your emotions become stuck? For, after all, a bad mood is nothing more than blocked emotions that normally flow within the relationship when there is a good spirit. So if you are in a bad mood, decide whom you are angry at. Check what has happened to your important relationships.

Are you angry at yourself? Is the brokenness in your relationship with self? If you are down on yourself, the bad mood may be part of a poor self-image. Could you be disappointed in yourself for some reason? Perhaps you got back into an old pattern that you despise about yourself. Perhaps you behaved just as your mother or father did and you promised you would never be like that. Or did you pass up some opportunity because you were unsure of yourself, and now you are kicking yourself for being so weak and indecisive? Or maybe you've been too hard on yourself, trying to be perfect and your self has become discouraged. If the precious relationship with self is broken, you can no longer feel deeply good about self. That puts you in a depressed mood.

Or are you angry at someone else? Is your bad mood coming from a stuck emotion that normally finds a home in someone else? Is there a brokenness between you and that other person? Do you feel their disrespect or their turning away from you? Perhaps your wife or husband gave you that "cut-down" look this morning and it hit home as you left the house to affect your mood all day long. Or perhaps someone recently showed you how disappointed they were in you. That would affect your spirits. Or, perhaps there is someone that comes to your mind often—someone you are yearning for, but things are just not right between the two of you. That would keep you in a low-level depression much of the time.

Or have you been disappointed again? Have you become disillusioned and now have nothing to believe in? Have you lost faith? Is your bad mood filled with cynicism and your brokenness a reflection of your lack of trust in life itself? Is the brokenness in your relationship with God? Is your energy for life itself blocked?

If at this moment you are in a bad mood, depressed, with no energy, it sounds as if you have a broken spirit. That means that at least one of your relationships has broken down and the emotional energy invested in it (the yearning) has been frustrated and blocked. Stuck emotion produces the mood.

The Two Paths

And what can you do about it? The decision is critical, because at this point there are two paths to follow. One will get you out of the mood quickly, but will do further damage to your relationships. This is the path of the bad spirit. You will always have the inclination to follow this path. The other path is more difficult because it initially hurts your pride. The other path is working on the broken relationship. The other path is the one back to the good spirit. Rita came to the choice between these two paths:

> So it was getting later and Derek was still not home from work. Rita shook her head as she looked at the clock. "I know he stopped for a drink on the way home again. Boy, will he have to pay when he gets in." He had done it to her again just after his promise to stop drinking. As she sat there fuming, Rita knew that Derek would only resent her more if she criticized him for drinking again, but she was feeling so hurt that she knew she would really rip into him as soon as he stepped in the door. He had broken her trust in him. Hers was a broken spirit.

Do you see the two paths? The more natural path for Rita would be to dump her anger and hurt on Derek and add more fuel to the vicious cycle of their relationship. She would get even and temporarily feel better. In fact her whole energy system would come alive as she tore into him. But that would be a destructive energy—a bad spirit—because it would perpetuate the destruction of their relationship. More hard feelings and greater brokenness would follow.

The other path for Rita is the more difficult one because it goes against the pride or the self-preservation instinct of the person. This is the path of forgiveness. This is the path that puts the relationship above self and sees the good spirit of the relationship as worth the struggle to attain it. This narrow path would require that Rita expose her brokenness to Derek *with the intention of helping their relationship,* not with the intention of making him feel guilty:

> Derek was already feeling guilty. He knew he would catch it when he walked in the door and he dreaded going home. He couldn't explain why he had stopped at the bar on the way home. He had promised Rita and himself that he would stop his drinking. He knew that it was tearing their marriage apart, especially when one drink led to another and then another. So defensively, he assumed an "I don't care" attitude as he walked through the door to an upset wife. But to his surprise, Rita did not go through the usual attack on his behavior, but said in a shaky voice, "I'm too upset and you're too drunk to handle this now. Let's talk about it in the morning."

Derek caught the note of hurt, yet also felt a genuine desire on Rita's part to work on their relationship. He felt that she wanted to do more than just criticize him. So now Derek was at a crossroad. He now had two paths to follow. His easiest path would be to forget about it in the morning and avoid Rita and the painful confrontation. He could act as if nothing happened and go off to work, insulating himself from the whole thing. But this path would be destructive by allowing the anger and unresolved hurt to fester at the intersection point of the marriage relationship. Though it would avoid painful contact for the moment, ignoring the feelings would not help restore the spirit of the relationship.

The narrow path would be difficult for Derek. To seek out the painful confrontation with a willingness to be open and vulnerable to Rita went against his nature. He would have to seek the confrontation *with the intention of working on the relationship*—with the intention of seeking help for the two of them, admitting a problem that could not be solved by quick promises and shallow apologies.

> The next morning Rita woke up with surprise. Derek was on the phone, asking to come into work a few hours late. She could hardly believe her eyes when he brought in coffee, sat down on the bed and, looking straight at her, said, "Rita, there is something very wrong between us. We need to do a lot of talking before it destroys our marriage." Her first impulse was to slip in a barb, like "I've been trying to tell you this for a long time." But Rita held back and said, with a note of appreciation in her voice, "I know there is, and I want to work on it, too."

The path toward reconciliation is not a natural path. True reconciliation takes place in a spirit of forgiveness. For confession is more than saying "I'm sorry"; and forgiveness is more than saying, "You're forgiven." The spirit of forgiveness puts the spirit of the relationship above self. The spirit of confession recognizes the sinful aspect of one's own humanness.

For Derek and Rita the spirit of confession was present in that each was willing to take a look at the way he or she contributed to the breakdown of the relationship. Such an attitude is a deep recognition of one's sinfulness and imperfection. It is a spirit of openness about one's failures and mixed motives—in the presence of the other person.

Confession is a deep recognition of the tainted nature of human beings. This shared attitude prepares the way for reconciliation. There can be no true, deep reconciliation without it. This takes away the destructive "win-lose" power struggle in which only pseudo-reconciliation occurs at the expense of the one who finally gives in. It also takes away the insulating truce that only covers up the hurt in a mutual agreement not to raise the painful issue.

The spirit of forgiveness was also present at that moment for Derek and Rita. As they faced each other, their relationship was more important than their individual hurts and pride.

Each was willing to acknowledge the other's hurt and to understand the reason for the other's actions. That is what reconciles. To see beyond one's hurt and recognize a basic integrity and worth in the other person is the essence of forgiveness.

God Forgives

This is the basis of God's forgiveness of us. As we recognize our fallenness, humanity, and deep need for something beyond our limited existence, he forgives. He understands our shortcomings and yet can see beyond our sinfulness to affirm a basic integrity and worth about our lives. He is willing to accept us, yearning for us to be reconciled to him. His forgiveness is based on his yearning for us to be in a relationship with him. This yearning is the same love that motivated God the Father to send his Son to redeem us.

God is willing to look past the lack of wholeness and fear that turned us away from him in the first place. He no longer enumerates our sins, but through Jesus Christ sees past our sin to the emptiness and anxiety that lie behind our sinfulness. He understands our need for him, and this understanding is a big part of his forgiveness. God weeps for us, yearning for us to hear his call, knowing that we "know not what we do."

Forgiving One's Self

And the same goes for being able to forgive one's self. Confession involves an understanding of one's limitations. It is the realization of our fallen nature and our inability to be perfect. It is an attitude of humility and readiness to acknowledge sin. It is allowing one's self to fail. Humility is having a down-to-earth view of one's own abilities and weaknesses. It is not having to take one's self so seriously; therefore we can break free from self-centeredness and ego-needs.

Such an attitude of confession toward self takes the pressure off. Instead of the two persons inside engaged in a power struggle, each can understand the other's needs.

The attitude of forgiveness toward self puts the relationship with self above one's accomplishments or self-gratification. It is the deep recognition that happiness comes from a good spirit within. It is the conviction that inner peace is worth more than fame, power, wealth, or reputation. The attitude of forgiveness is the willingness to see beyond the hurt of failure to the anxiety that brought about the weakness in self. It is the commitment to love self—to continually work on that precious relationship from which the good spirit emerges.

But, for that attitude to be present, there must be a basis for such trust. There must be something for one's consciousness to be organized around. The true starting point is the love of God—the Holy Spirit building a temple inside one's heart. Our identity as children of God reassures us of his constant love for us. This identity is the starting point for confession and forgiveness.

Once that relationship is intact and you have something to deeply believe in, then you need not take yourself so seriously. Then things fall into perspective and you are no longer driven by a passion for success or for pleasure. You are now free to understand yourself and forgive, as God has forgiven you. With this freedom I have a confession to make:

> A number of people, including many of my counselees, have wondered how I stay so calm and can usually shift easily into their world as I listen to them. Part of that, I am not proud to say, is my defense that keeps me insulated from personal attacks. But there is a part of that peacefulness that is genuine. There is a basic attitude inside that recognizes my own limitations and forgives the blunders and mixed motives. I know that this attitude comes from the work of the Holy Spirit within me. My relationship with God is not all that perfect and this attitude comes and goes. But through it all, I know there is something deeply there that allows me to test the limits. There is a freedom in my identity as a child of God that is real, though hard to put into words. I don't have to play God in my counseling—it is his Spirit that recreates the good spirit in that person, so I can forgive myself for bumbling or satisfying my own ego for the moment. It just is not up to me to heal. That is beyond my power. Further, a

deep knowledge that I am, through it all, one of God's own gives a perspective to my life. I do not have to take my life and work that seriously. There can be a lightness and a twinkle in my eye even when things get heavy in the counseling. What are all of these struggles as compared to the depth that a relationship with God gives to life? And, even more important, God gives a source of hope when everything else seems hopeless. The best way I can tell it is that when I have felt everything gone—when my job, my identity, and my security were stripped away, there was still something there —something that no one could take away.

As I think back over that time in my life, I know that I was not as aware of how the two deepest relationships in my life were so much a part of my identity. Nor was I aware of the depth of the strength these relationships gave to my life. But, when the chips were down, there was really something there that took away a lot of the hurt and fear: my family, especially my wife Kathy, and the Holy Spirit.

It was a source of energy that I could feel beneath everything else. It was a wellspring of energy from those two spirits that kept my spirits alive. I knew that I could be in good spirits again even though my own career and self-identity were shaken up.

A Close Look at a Broken Spirit

Betty's spirit was broken. She put her hands over her face as if the deep shame kept her from being able to face anyone. She couldn't believe that she did it and felt a deep hatred for herself at the moment. The scene flashed back into her mind. A few drinks at the beach with her girl friend, feeling so angry at her husband for not taking time off to join her, feeling deeply lonely and unloved, meeting a handsome caring person, talking half of the night, feeling so close and understood—but her mind stopped there. It was too painful to go on. She felt like dirt. How could she have allowed herself to become sexually involved with him? It went against all of her morals—against her deep promise to herself to remain faithful to her husband. She just couldn't face him again—couldn't face anyone again. She couldn't trust herself anymore. In fact, it seemed as if she didn't know herself anymore and, almost as if to punish herself, the picture of what she did flashed back into her mind again and again. She had nothing but contempt for herself.

Do you see how Betty is fighting herself? Her brokenness is really the relationship with self that was destroyed by the way she went against her values. Her sexual experience deeply hurt the logical person ("head") inside, breaking down her self-image. Her reputation and her image were tarnished. She went against what she believed in, and she was so angry at herself. The anger showed itself in disgust, guilt, and depression. It was anger turned inward. Betty's energy was blocked —turned in on itself. She was trapped in her emotional experience with her relationship with self broken. Death, at times, seemed the only way out.

But her brokenness did not occur overnight. Her relationship with self had been breaking down for some time. Her emotional side ("heart") had been hurting in her marriage for years, but her "head" had been covering up the hurt with excuses and idealization. She did not let herself realize the depth of her loneliness and frustration, but pretended to be happy and put on a good show to others. So her "heart" had taken a beating and was not being heard. Her image for a long time was more important than deep happiness inside.

So, even though Betty's "head" felt OK before the affair, her "heart" was almost totally crushed. Her hurt and anger toward her husband was all pent up inside. She was dying inside, and the affair was born out of her depression. It was a desperate cry for help, a move of desperation in her relationship with her husband and in her relationship with herself. But it only left her disgusted with herself and unable to face her husband.

"Can I ever be in good spirits again?" Betty asked herself over and over. At that moment it seemed to her that all hope was gone and thoughts of dying lingered in her mind. This was Betty last year.

Take a look at Betty today. There is a deep feeling of peace inside, and she and her husband are closer than they have ever been. But that did not happen overnight.

Betty began the slow, painful process of rebuilding those relationships. She was tempted to give up, stay depressed and adopt a careless attitude. Her moods flipped back and forth from feeling horribly guilty and worthless to feeling, "Who cares, anyway?" Her moods were ripping her apart, and she was ready for help.

The first step in rebuilding her relationships was honesty (the attitude of confession). She admitted her brokenness to herself. Her "heart" admitted the hurt in the way it had chosen to deal with the growing loneliness. Her "head" admitted putting down and covering up her emotional needs. She stopped putting herself down and started getting to know herself.

And she confessed to her husband. She stopped covering up the brokenness of their relationship and opened up to him. She risked his revenge and sarcasm. She confessed in the spirit of trying to help their relationship.

And she saw past her own hurt to forgive herself—to understand the loneliness that had brought her to do this. It took months of raising the issues, of getting out the old anger, of struggling with some powerful moods for the healing to occur. But the good spirits gradually came back and with it Betty's energy for living. Through the process of honesty and putting the spirit of the relationship above self, the broken spirits were healed. Betty was in good spirits again!

10

Dealing with Bad Spirits—

Confrontation

There is no sense in being nice to a bad spirit. Such a spirit must be broken first in order to be put together right. If the spirit is still a bad spirit, reconciliation cannot take place. So long as the bad spirit is still around, it will win out in the long run.

Discerning the Spirits

How then does one go about breaking a bad spirit? In the Old Testament, the prophets pointed out the evil in the world about them. Confronting bad spirits has always been a part of the prophetic function of the church. This is not to be done by self-appointed prophets who crusade against what they in a self-righteous way consider evil, but rather by people of God who see evil also at work in themselves. It's hard to clearly discern a bad spirit in someone else when your own vision is blurred by a bad spirit inside, tainted by your selfish motives. To illustrate, it does little good to point out the sin of an unmarried couple living together if it makes you feel righteous in doing so. You've got your own bad spirit to deal with first. It's hard to see the mote in another's eye if you have a beam in your own eye (Matt. 7:3).

So the starting point, as always, is the Word of God. This Word tells us that *all* have sinned and fallen short. This is the basis of humility—to see ourselves as under the mighty hand of God, needing his forgiveness. Let me take a look at my own humanity:

> I don't like to think of myself as needing help. I am a good person, dedicated to the profession of helping others, and I can rationalize my motives for counseling as being completely pure—for the helping of others. But in a moment of honesty I can see the bad spirits kicking around. My commitment to the welfare of others is tainted by motives of earning more money or of building a good reputation. I'm not as pure as I would like to think or as I would like others to think. My motives are mixed, and it hurts to admit that. The bad spirit within would tempt me to keep up the good front—to justify charging my clients because "it makes them take the counseling more seriously." Or that spirit would tempt me to rationalize a failure as, "It was evident that they really didn't want to work on their marriage after all." It is tempting for me to idealize my counseling by pointing to my successes. I have my share of bad spirits!

So the place to start with the confrontation is with self. The place to start is with confession. Confession, after all, is good for your soul. It cleanses the soul from the false ways of fitting things together—from our rationalizations, justifications, and idealizations. Confession involves admitting our sinful human nature. It is the admission that we have tainted our motives and kidded ourselves about the purity of our lives. It is the simple statement, "God, be merciful to me, a sinner" (Luke 18:13).

So how does one recognize a bad spirit? Evil is going against God's will—going against what it takes to relate to God, others, and self. The first thing, then, to look for is energy that seems to be directed toward an evil purpose—energy used to tear down some person or relationship. If "good" can be summarized as the "building up" process of Christian love, then evil can be summarized as the opposite. So energy "hell-bent" towards tearing down these relationships is a bad spirit.

To recognize a bad spirit is to discern the evil purpose of the energy, to *name* the spirit. A bad spirit can go about its destructive ways unhindered if it is not named. A bad spirit can even hide behind the rationalizations and pose as a good spirit. Barbara thought her motives were right at first:

> Barbara knew that there were a lot of drugs passed around at the high school and began to fear that her daughter would start experimenting. Barbara tried to be subtle about it, but the fear was on her mind all the time. She began to watch her daughter's behavior closely, looking for symptoms. She went through her daughter's room during the day, looking for clues and reading all notes she found in the room, including the diary that was kept carefully locked. Barbara always found enough that seemed to justify her suspicions and keep her looking. After all, she was trying to protect her child from the evil influences at the high school.

Could you name the bad spirit in Barbara's case? Was it the availability of drugs in high school? Even though drug abuse has potential demonic effects, the bad spirit in Barbara's case was her *suspicion* and *distrust* of her daughter. Why was this evil? So much of Barbara's energy was devoted to activity that kept driving a wedge deeper and deeper between the two of them. Barbara would find things to fuel her suspicions, and these would make her distrust her daughter more and more. She was setting herself up to view her daughter negatively. A burst of teenage energy immediately set off Barbara's fears. It became more and more difficult to see past her fears and enjoy her relationship with her daughter.

Her daughter, in return, felt her mother's distrust and became more and more secretive. She resented her lack of privacy and began to lose the openness she once had with her mother. It seemed that anything she would be open about would lead to more investigation, so she carefully kept things from her mother. Barbara became convinced that her daughter was hiding something and searched even harder. Finally the thought started popping into her daughter's head, "Well, I might as well try using drugs since I am going to be accused of it anyway."

So Barbara's obsessive fear of drugs and her distrust of her daughter turned out to be a bad spirit. This spirit was camouflaged quite well in Barbara's concern for her daughter's welfare. Gradually the destructive nature of the spirit emerged as their relationship grew worse and worse.

It was easy to see and name the bad spirit by the time the relationship between mother and daughter had been destroyed. The bad spirit was evident in their distrust, resentment, and hatred toward each other. But how could such a bad spirit be confronted before it totally destroyed the relationship? Simply put, how does one discern evil from good?

Sources of Help

There are three sources of help in discerning and naming a bad spirit: God's Word, the law written in our hearts, and the Christian community.

Since God's law is really the basis for discernment, his Word to us cuts through our attempts to kid ourselves. We learn of the powerful, destructive potential of spreading rumors from the commandment, "Thou shalt not bear false witness." We also learn from examples of communities destroyed by factions as recorded in Scriptures (1 Cor. 1:13). We can discern the demonic potential of the misplaced sexual drive from the commandment, "Thou shalt not commit adultery," and from the stories of King David and others. We know of the evil consequences of anger allowed to build up from the commandment, "Thou shalt not kill," and from the example of Cain and Abel.

It is a Word from the Creator. He knows us so well and cares so much for us that he let us in on his purpose for creation. And more than that, he points out again and again the consequences of succumbing to a bad spirit, providing concrete examples again and again in his Word. And it is this

Word, like a "two-edged sword," that can cut through our rationalizations, justifications, and idealizations. With this Word, we can name the bad spirits with confidence.

Since his law is written in our hearts and vibrates within our souls, we also know something is wrong by that still, small voice within us that won't let us rest. As we listen to this voice and value its message, we also receive help in naming the bad spirit:

> Barbara started waking up at 4:00 A.M. It was unusual for her not to be able to sleep. After about a week of troubled sleep, she began to realize that something was deeply wrong with her life. There was a small voice inside that was trying to tell her something. Then suddenly she knew what it was. She and Keith were drifting apart after five years of marriage, but she had been covering it up in her mind. Now that she felt the neglect of their relationship, she felt a strong attraction and fantasy toward other men. It was the strength of this fantasy that disturbed her sleep. She could no longer ignore that she and Keith were dangerously far away from each other.

Barbara had rationalized the lack of communication in their marriage. She excused his long hours at work and had gotten into the habit of falling asleep before Keith came to bed because she just needed more sleep than he did. But these excuses were covering over the brokenness and allowing the marriage to break down even further. The still small voice inside called her to honesty.

There is yet a third source for help in naming a bad spirit. Often we get so wrapped up in our own logic and idealization that we are blind to the destructive path we have taken. At that time we need others to confront us. They can name a bad spirit from their perspective far better than we can. This is one of the functions of the Christian community. The community of believers is instructed to admonish one another.

King David had found a way to live with his conscience, rationalizing his affair with Bathsheba. It took someone else to speak the harsh word to him, cutting through his defenses and bringing him to the point of brokenness and repentance. The prophet Nathan confronted him, named his evil spirit, and broke through to him. David could now be whole again. Through repentance and forgiveness, he could once again be in good spirits!

Before Nathan confronted him, David was a troubled man. He did not feel deeply good inside, and the bad spirit made him do more and more things to cover up his adulterous actions. He had lost his good spirit, and deep inside, David knew it.

This account of Nathan's confrontation of King David in 2 Sam. 12:1-20 teaches us much about dealing with bad spirits. It shows that a bad spirit must become a broken spirit. For the good spirit to come back—for David to be able to feel deeply good about himself again—his spirit had to be brought back to the starting point of the brokenness. David had to face and confess what it was that originally broke down his good spirit. This is always a painful process.

David was apparently lonely, yearning for closeness as he saw Bathsheba bathing on the rooftop. The temptation was strong, and he justified to himself the affair he had with her. But when the affair threatened to become exposed because of Bathsheba's pregnancy, a bad spirit took over and did more than justify. In his desperation, he manipulated her husband to get him to think it was his own child. When the manipulation did not work, David finally justified having him killed in the front lines of battle. David became a monster as the bad spirit tried more and more desperately to cover up his affair.

No matter how powerful his bad spirit was, the pull of the right spirit was yet more powerful. Nathan's confrontation hit home. David was brought back to the point where his good spirit had originally been broken. Nathan cut through all the rationalizations and justifications with the simple statement, "You are the man." A flood of emotion came over the king as his soul was bared. He repented—feeling the ugliness of his sin. His evil spirit was broken. He had "a broken and contrite heart," and God did not despise or forsake David in his brokenness.

Confronting in the Right Spirit

In order to be effective, such confrontation by others must be made in the right spirit. Nathan's intention in confronting his king was to help David get his good spirit back. His intention was to help and restore, not to break the king down, to blackmail him, or to seek revenge. In order to be effective, the intention in any confrontation must be to restore that good spirit.

Such confrontation can so easily come from one's own ego needs or from a subtle desire to cut the person down. Such *evil* intention will always make the confrontation ineffective in restoring a good spirit. It will only produce more brokenness and give the person's bad spirit more fuel for its activity. Cindy did not confront in the right spirit:

"I knew it!" Cindy shouted, almost with satisfaction. She had just found some pornography in her son's room after accusing him many times of looking at such things. He had denied it again and again, but now she had proof. So she marched right up to the den where her son was watching T.V. "So, you've been lying all along," Cindy began, "and now I have proof." As she laid into him, there was a sense of being in control that she liked. She had him where she wanted him.

Even though Cindy was "right," her intention in confronting her son made her confrontation ineffective. In fact, her actions added more fuel to his bad spirit. He perceived her desire to put him down, and he resented her even more. The confrontation did little for his spirit and absolutely nothing for the spirit of their relationship.

So, again, any confrontation of others begins with self. One's own bad spirits will always produce mixed motives for opening up an issue. So you notice your daughter getting too serious with her boyfriend at age 15. Is it the hurt of losing her, or is

it concern for her welfare that prompts your words with her?
So your wife seems to be drinking too much. Is it the family
image, or is it concern for what must be happening to her that
prompts you to raise the issue? For, you see, the helpfulness
of the confrontation of one by another depends on the spirit
in which the issue is raised. Confrontation will seldom restore
a good spirit if the issue is raised in the wrong spirit.

But why confess? After all, it is painful to admit one's weakness—to bare one's soul. So why go through such a heartrending process? Because there is hope that one's soul can still be
touched and hope that there can actually be a good spirit
recreated out of the brokenness.

Now it is time for confession again. Pause for a moment and
see if you can bare your own soul. What needs confronting in
your own life? What is it that keeps you from being in good
spirits? What is it that is deeply troubling you? Has that
small voice been trying to get your attention? Close your eyes
for a minute and give this voice a chance. What has taken over
your life? What has broken down in your life?

PART FOUR

OVERCOMING TODAY'S SPIRITUAL PROBLEMS

The Christian message does not change. People remain sinful, and God's law is applicable to all generations. Our need for a Savior also is changeless as the gospel rings true from age to age.

But the devil changes the rules of the game! His ways of presenting temptation and the rationalizations, justifications, and idealizations that pop so easily into our minds are subtle parts of the culture of each age. As history teaches us, the paths that seem so innocent and justifiable actually lead to destruction.

And so the prophetic task of the church in any age is to call into question the life-styles and paths that seem harmless or easily rationalized. With this in mind, the remaining chapters of this book look at our own age. What is it, in practice, that nurses the demons and gives fuel to bad spirits today? What are the typical rationalizations our culture offers that seem to soothe broken spirits? What idealizations seem to perpetuate the demonic?

Several principles provide the guiding rationale for the chapters. First, God's Law remains the standard for recognizing potential bad spirits. Second, the example of Scripture provides the method for confronting these spirits. Further, the starting point for any confrontation is with one's own mixed motives. It is backward to look for the bad spirits "out there" before confronting them within.

The purpose of these chapters is not to put down any person, life-style, or group; nor is the purpose to grind any axes. The purpose is to enable all of us who are deeply caught up in our culture and its temptations to confront these spirits so that we can be in good spirits.

11

The Spirit of the Age

The best phrase to express the spirit of our age is "fast relief." Our age espouses instant intimacy, quick solutions, and fast relief from anything unpleasant. The message from an endless barrage of commercials is the quick cure or the painless solution. A product is judged better if it offers a faster or more powerful way to become attractive, get rid of headaches, or achieve happiness.

The spirit of the age is thus opposed to what it takes to establish deep relationships. This spirit destroys what it takes to be in good spirits. It takes the depth out of our lives, producing a "problem-free," banal existence. It's no wonder that boredom and apathy reign. There is just not much to get deeply excited about. So, in the absence of deep feelings in one's life, one struggles to find excitement. For some, this struggle becomes obsessive—a demonic driving force in many lives. The search for the ultimate experience or the best orgasm drives people to do strange things!

Depersonalization

What happened to leave so many people lonely, bored, unfulfilled, and vaguely anxious about their lives? What happened was an *insulation* of the deep emotions in the effort to better control one's life. Or, in a word, what happened was *depersonalization.*

The roots of depersonalization go back a long way. As with so many trends, it began quite innocently. Centuries ago the philosopher Descartes suggested that a person could be divided into mind and body with the mind capable of exploring and controlling the body. He did this for a "Christian" purpose, suggesting that God's image in us was really our minds. This philosophy, dualism, helped open the way for objective analysis and the scientific advances that use that method (the scientific method) of looking at the world. The Puritan era towards the end of the last century added to this dualism by suggesting that the mind's control over the body impulses was "godliness."

And now, during the last several decades, advances in scientific technology have taken this philosophy to its extreme. Objectivity and change are seen as good within the probing style of scientific research. Truth has become equated with objective data. The computer, which can organize and analyze vast amounts of this "truth," has become the hero of the age.

Subtly, as the life-style of our day took on the form of the computer, an element of human life started disappearing. The computer can get the job done and make precise decisions in record time, but who can relate to a computer? By using the computer as a model for life, our culture began sacrificing its ability to form deep and permanent relationships. Being objective and open to change are traits that translate easily into a detachable personality. Insulation and superficiality are the inevitable results.

In order to stay detached and objective, scientists must not get emotionally involved and thus contaminate their data. They must become and remain depersonalized. And all of that necessary insulation between their "logical" and their "emotional" persons inside makes them less and less capable of deep relationships within self and with others. Let me illustrate with a personal example:

Most of my education seemed bent on teaching me how to detach and insulate myself. Analysis and objectivity were the key words, especially in graduate school. I learned well the research model and even got into computer programming to analyze the wealth of data my dissertation produced. But that took its toll on my personality. It became easier and easier for me to insulate myself from what was going on in the present. I could easily be talking to Kathy or be in some other social situation, but have my mind somewhere else. I could control my emotional reactions also. If I felt some emotional reaction (like anger), I would use a little trick of the mind. I would go into neutral and drain the emotion away. I was "logical" again with no fear of "losing control" and "contaminating" the situation with emotion. I am a product of this age and have been carefully trained to insulate myself and become more like the "god" of this age, the computer. I learned well!

Kathy, I am happy to say, has broken through much of this insulation and stirred up the deep, relating emotions in me. But it is an ongoing struggle in my life. All it takes is some intensive research, computer programming, or writing a book, and I revert and become detached and inaccessible again. My capacity to relate then suffers.

The Computer Personality

The "computer personality" of our scientific age is similar to the "schizoid" personality that Rollo May found increasingly common in his work as a psychiatrist. One's heart—with its deep emotions, private hopes, and dreams—is kept carefully insulated from significant involvement with the interactions of daily life. A person is able to "plug in and plug out" of situations without much trouble. Commitment and depth become difficult. Deep relationships are hard to come by.

There are at least six ways in which the personality modeled after the computer has affected life within our society. All six work against the spirit by seriously affecting the ability of people to form deep relationships. The result is feelings of loneliness, alienation, and boredom, and a growing desperate search for something missing from life, making people vulnerable to a bad spirit.

1. The model of the computer stresses *objectivity*. The "computer" personality as shown above is trained to build a wall around the heart in order to keep feelings, hopes, wishes, and dreams from contaminating the data. Yet these are the very things on which a relationship thrives. If the heart is kept guarded from the relationship, the interaction can only be superficial. Good relationships are *subjective* and defy detached analysis. They cannot be talked about; they must be experienced.

2. There is also an *impermanence* in this computer model of personality. People find it easy to walk away from relationships—unplugging themselves when things get tense. Such impermanence makes commitment, which is so vital to deep relationships, impossible. Temporary arrangements seem more practical than permanent marriages.

3. A computer personality allows for easy *mobility*. If a person does not sink roots down into a community, it is easy to move if a better job becomes available. With about 40% of the society on the move every five years, this disruptive pressure upon relationships with others is ever-present.

4. The life-style of the scientific age is *fragmented*. The computer personality can easily move from situation to situation by using another plug. It is easy to adjust to the requirements of the environment and to become the person needed for the situation (to become reprogrammed). It is easy to be many different people.

5. TV and other mass media make us all *spectators;* the communication is one-way. It can be turned off at will. If there is some tension between people, they can easily ignore the other. Each member of the family goes its own way.

6. The speed at which the computer personality can change or be reprogrammed makes it easy for people to misunderstand each other. In the age of *accelerated change,* couples without in-depth contact can wake up strangers. They no

longer understand one another and cannot be open in the relationship. It also makes it difficult to know yourself.

The computer personality is not happy with life. The trail of superficial relationships takes its toll, and the soul yearns for fulfillment. *Boredom* and *loneliness* rob the person of life. The deep emotions cry out for expression, and the search is on for something that is missing.

Devaluation

This frustration erupts in many forms. The result of depersonalization is devaluation. And virtually everyone belongs to some group that feels depersonalized. Everyone feels labeled and to some degree treated as a number or an object. Women feel used by men—objects for their depersonalized sexual conquest. Consumers feel cynical toward "personalized" messages from a form letter, knowing that despite the pretense of concern, the real goal is to persuade you to buy some product. We end up so often feeling used, and therefore unimportant. We are just a number to so many companies, agencies, and people. And this breaks our spirits!

The constant put-downs, feelings of loneliness, and of a lack of caring lie smoldering under the controlled facade of the personality. The deep anger and frustration that this produces is demon-fuel, ready to erupt in inappropriate ways. I encountered one of these demons on the highway:

> I was driving along the highway several days ago and came to a place where two lanes had to merge into one. I was not paying close enough attention to the situation and realized that another car was at the merger-point also. Trying to make the best of the situation, I sped up to give him room to slip in behind me. He easily made it, but had to slow up a little to do it. This slight inconvenience erupted in almost violent anger. Through the rear view mirror I saw him shake his fist and yell what seemed to be a string of obscenities. He then proceeded to ride my bumper for a number of miles, knuckles white on his steering wheel, trying to scare me.

Smoldering frustration erupting into violence—that is a good indication of some of today's demons. These demons are fueled by depersonalized messages ever-present in our culture. The person wants to be acknowledged, to be noticed and taken into account. Perhaps the worst feeling anyone can have in our culture is, "If I died today, no one would really miss me. I just don't matter that deeply to anyone."

Predictably a new spirit has developed in our age to counter and soothe the brokenness or depersonalization. This new spirit falls under the title of *humanism* and seeks to give a feeling of personal importance by encouraging the person to feel good about self as an individual. And for the persons feeling the brokenness of their superficial relationships, it is tempting to pull back into their selves and find worth in being alive and in being human.

But the path inward can produce only a shallow, "I'm OK." For the person turned in on self, the feeling of worth does not go deep enough. The depth of a good spirit relates to the depth of the relationship. In contrast to God's deep love for us in Jesus Christ, the smiling "I'm OK" is pathetically shallow.

So this humanistic philosophy can lead to a bad spirit because it leads to more brokenness. Carrying this philosophy to an extreme, one can justify breaking a relationship whenever it is not happy and fulfilling. One form of this philosophy assumes that you deserve to be happy at all times. Thus you have the right to discard anything that is painful or has an element of struggle in it. This path is not the path to deep relationships, which require the daily struggle and painful confrontation so characteristic of the Christian spirit.

So the brokenness you and I experience today lies in the superficial quality of our lives—in the shallowness and insulation that takes the life out of our relationships. Our culture has a serious spiritual problem. So many people cannot form and maintain deep, personal relationships with others, with self, or with God. Such is the toll of our computerized society.

Breaking Through

How can one be in good spirits again against such odds? Contact, commitment, daily confession and forgiveness are still the way to a good spirit. Breaking through the insulation comes by asking the searching question, "Who are you?" To confront the blockage and become vulnerable again, putting the relationship above the comforts of self, is the slow, sometimes painful, move toward that good spirit.

It is the same with the demons that wake us up at 3:00 A.M. —that trouble our sleep and drive us to further insulation by pills and medication. We know that things are not right in our souls, but we have become so detached from our souls that we often do not know what is really bothering us. In prayer and confession we bare our souls, and through God's forgiveness our lives are repersonalized. Personalization and wholeness, then, are God's gifts to us who so often feel small. Look at Christ's response to Zacchaeus, who felt small and insignificant:

> He entered Jericho and was passing through. And there was a man named Zacchaeus; he was a chief tax collector, and rich. And he sought to see who Jesus was, but could not, on account of the crowd, because he was small of stature. So he ran on ahead and climbed up into a sycamore tree to see him, for he was to pass that way. And when Jesus came to the place, he looked up and said to him, "Zacchaeus, make haste and come down; for I must stay at your house today." So he made haste and came down, and received him joyfully. And when they saw it, they all murmured, "He has gone in to be the guest of a man who is a sinner." And Zacchaeus stood and said to the Lord, "Behold, Lord, the half of my goods I give to the poor; and if I have defrauded anyone of anything, I restore it fourfold." And Jesus said to him, "Today salvation has come to this house, since he also is a son of Abraham. For the Son of man came to seek and to save the lost" (Luke 19:1-10).

God sees us in the personal way he saw Zacchaeus. We are

not just a number in his heavenly computer. His Holy Spirit dwells in our hearts, and we are worth something. We have been repersonalized as God's children.

12

Dealing with Alcohol "Spirits" and Drug "Demons"

Alcoholism and drug addiction are spiritual problems. They are chemical ways of imitating a good spirit. They are spiritual problems because the addiction usually arises from a feeling of brokenness in some relationship (with self, others, and/or God) and usually ends up further destroying the spirit of these relationships.

These bad spirits are so dangerous because they so closely imitate a good spirit. Whenever a painful struggle with self occurs, the bad mood that goes along with this struggle can be instantly changed by any number of chemical substances. There can be an instant mood change—instant peace with self. Or so it seems. The only difference between this spirit and a *good* spirit is that with the chemical spirit not *all* of the person is "high." Eventually the deep realization comes that these "good" feelings are not part of a good relationship, but that they are drug-induced. This realization further tends to break down the relationship with self:

> Ann's mood quickly changed. She knew she needed to study, but a restlessness hit her. "I guess I'm just not in the mood to study," she thought and was aware of the struggle going on

inside. Part of her (her head) felt the need to hit the books, but something deep was gnawing away at her. All she could think about was the party going on. She tried to fight her impulse to go, but suddenly a different mood hit. "The test will be impossible anyway, so why try?" As that thought ran through her mind, she no longer felt like fighting the impulse. The next thing she knew, she was at the party. Once there, she quickly looked for the drinks and scarcely talked to anyone as she downed her first one. She grabbed a second, almost with a note of desperation—and then she relaxed as that good old warm feeling started spreading inside. There was still a vague feeling of guilt for not studying, but now she was feeling too good to care. Not too much mattered anymore as she quickly followed with her third and fourth glasses.

In a sense, Ann was an alcoholic. She knew that a few drinks would change her mood and she had begun to rationalize her dependency on it. The first time she took a drink back in high school, she felt its power. She got a warmth inside she had never experienced before. The warmth took away the constant bad feelings and emptiness that she seemed to carry with her ever since she could remember. Now, four years later, much of her college life was planned around drinking. It was the only sure way to get her back into a "good mood."

But, when she finally came in to see me—almost dragged in by her scared friends after she blacked out during a night of heavy drinking—even she knew that something was terribly wrong with her. She had lost all self-respect and was quite depressed. She couldn't trust herself, knowing that at the first excuse, she would be out drinking again. Her relationship with herself was broken: she hated what she had become, but felt totally helpless to do anything about it. She had promised herself countless times that she would stop drinking, only to find herself drunk again the very same day. She had lost her willpower. All of her energy was turned against herself. She wanted to die.

And that's the way it is with a bad spirit. Drinking seemed innocent enough at first, and she was sure she could control it.

"After all, what good is a party unless you feel good? Besides, I deserve to feel good a few times in my life." This was the bad spirit talking, giving her the rationalization she needed to continue drinking. It was *evil* because it further destroyed her relationships. Her parents lost trust in her, and there were endless battles over her going out. Her friends lost respect for her, and she gradually lost her own freedom and willpower. Her drinking became demonic—a driving force in her life that was ever-present. She had no choice. She had to have a drink. She had become an alcoholic.

Our Drug Culture

Even though drug-related demons are not unique to our culture, they do reflect the spirit of the age. Drugs represent a way of controlling emotions and behavior. They go along with the way the "computer personality" of our day insulates itself from deeper problems and conflicts. Ours is a "drug culture" that doesn't think twice about altering moods or handling tension by a chemical means. The doctor's prescriptions are seldom questioned, and innumerable drugs are promoted legally in commercials that offer instant relief.

So the spirit of the age promotes and justifies the superficial, instant good feeling that chemicals can give. We would be incensed if a doctor let someone stay in pain when the pain could be so easily relieved by a shot of Demerol. No one should be made to suffer. With this cultural justification, it is an easy step to addiction. "What's wrong with feeling good? I have a right to feel that way, don't I?" So, in our age, rationalizations and justifications abound for "getting high."

But, as with all bad spirits, the reason for taking drugs in the first place no longer remains the reason for continuing. This is when the demon emerges! Drinking and pill-taking become driving forces in their own right. The desire for the substance is now a driving force—a demon. Concern for adequate supplies of alcohol or of pills becomes obsessive.

Thoughts of the next opportunity for getting high constantly crowd into consciousness. The person is possessed!

Does that mean that drugs are evil? Of course not! They are part of God's creation and are good. But, as in everything, the devil can take what God intended for good and use it for his evil purposes. The mind-set of our culture makes it easy for the devil to pop easy justification into our heads for abuse of drugs.

Abuse and Addiction

How can you tell when abuse starts? Are you vulnerable to addiction? Abuse is present whenever the drug becomes an important part of your life. If you have trouble giving up the good feelings it produces; if you begin planning things around the drug; and if any obsessive thought or action surrounds your use of the drug, then you are vulnerable to addiction.

I've also found that a person is vulnerable to addiction if there is a significant personality or mood change when under the influence of the drug. A person who usually gives in to others when sober and becomes aggressive when drinking is a likely candidate for addiction. A person whose depression turns into expressions of energy and excitement after a few drinks is another likely candidate. Sylvia was just such a candidate:

> Sylvia seemed to be responding to therapy nicely. She acknowledged that she had a drinking problem and was interested in taking steps to solve it. She knew that her drinking was a way to escape from deep feelings of loneliness, but did not want to use that escape anymore. I was beginning to feel good about her resolve until she was walking out of my office. A strange look came over her face and with a sly smile that negated everything else to that point, she said, "You'll probably be tired of me before it's all over."

The other person inside had emerged and knew that the resolves would never be kept. Her "head" was serious about wanting to assert her willpower and quit drinking. She was convinced that she "should" quit. But the other side knew better, and the sly smile was the other person inside her talking. Her "heart" knew the resolve would weaken when the loneliness hit again and that within the next few days she would be drunk again:

> Sylvia walked out of my office determined to stop drinking, but felt a deep depression come over her at the thought. She tried to push it out of her mind, but thoughts of a nice stiff drink kept popping back into her head. The depression grew, and she phoned a friend in desperation to keep her from slipping. But when there was no answer, something inside said: "No one cares anyway, so why not feel better? After all, one drink won't hurt anything." That sly smile appeared on her face again as she got out her favorite glass. In a few minutes she would be feeling better again. The other voice inside tried to remind her of the resolve, but that voice was ignored. The drink was already half-consumed. A half hour later when her friend called, there was no sign of the depression. There was now only joking and laughter. She was a different Sylvia.

A person who feels deeply good about self is not that vulnerable to addiction. If the person has a good relationship with self, there is a good spirit and little chance for such a personality change when drinking. But whenever one's good spirit breaks down and the person splits more and more into two people, the likelihood for this critical mood shift becomes greater.

One of the things that makes it difficult to work with an addict is that all too often you are dealing with the two people inside at odds with each other. The person can make all sorts of promises when sober and actually mean them, but not be able to carry through as the other side begins to take over. Alcoholics then appear to be con artists, not to be trusted in any of their promises. The whole process, as with all bad spirits, then gets into a demonic vicious cycle. Upon sobering up, the other side becomes remorseful and depressed. Then comes the escalation. When drinking occurs and the "I don't care" attitude becomes stronger, the person's remorse also has to become stronger when the person is sober. But the "belittled" feelings then build up more powerfully to explode when the drinking recurs again. The result of this demonic cycle is pathetic, as all relationships in the person's life break down. There is no longer any spirit for life. They have sold their soul to the devil. Alcohol becomes the only reason for living.

Addictions Arising Out of the Relationship with Self

Guilt-related addiction. The alcohol or drug addict who is filled with remorse and self-depreciation when sober is a good example of this type. The person was usually raised with a feeling inside that something is bad about him. Cliff felt this way about himself:

> Cliff could never remember being happy with himself. He had an ugly feeling deep down, never feeling that he was good enough. Whatever he did, his father would criticize. He could never please him. It was just like a deep hurt—deeper than he could express. Whenever he did anything wrong, he would punish himself by thinking over his fault again and again. His "head" would endlessly arouse his guilt. He felt totally worthless as a human being. Then he was introduced to alcohol one evening when he was extremely depressed, and for the first time since he could remember, the ugly feeling inside became mellow. It was still there, but something smoothed it over, and for the first time, he wasn't thinking about what he had done wrong. As he got louder and livelier, he didn't care about pleasing anyone. There was a beautiful fog where the guilt and pain used to be.

Cliff was raised in a high-guilt environment. His parents did not mean to, but their concern over raising him "right" had them, especially his father, constantly correcting his faults.

So Cliff got the message that he was not good enough, that his parents were disappointed in him. Guilt was such a familiar emotion that even the thought of doing something they might disapprove of aroused a twinge in his stomach. So he was a "good boy" and never did anything much wrong, but he felt guilty all the time.

His guilt represented a brokenness inside. His "head" was trying to be perfect in a desperate attempt to please his parents. That pitted this side against his "heart" and its emotional needs. His feelings and impulses were immediately put down by his "head," which used guilt to stay in control. He was so often at war with himself, with his energy blocked, that his spirit was broken.

He was a prime candidate for something that would produce warmth and a good feeling inside. And alcohol released this energy—giving a feeling of peace. From that moment on, Cliff wanted that feeling again. He had found a way to have a "good" spirit and the temptation became overpowering after that. A demon was born within, and his life gradually became more and more centered around the next opportunity to drink. Driven by this powerful force, he became a teenage alcoholic.

Anxiety-based addiction. The addict who is fearful and anxious about life when straight is an example of this type of addict. The anxiety comes from a poor relationship with self and the feeling of poor control over one's impulses. This person does not trust self and experiences a high level of mood swings. The anxiety usually signals the approach of a situation in which there will be opposing feelings from the person's "head" and "heart." Pam often felt that anxiety:

> Pam felt it coming on again. The quivering was starting up inside, and she could feel herself falling apart. She had so much trouble making decisions and felt so helpless inside. The anxiety was horrible and would build up so much that sometimes she couldn't leave her house. She hated that scared feeling inside. Her mother took her to a doctor when her anxiety showed up in lower abdominal pains. Finding

nothing physically wrong, he prescribed Valium. And the first one she took made such a difference! She could function again, and the shaking inside was smoothed over. But one Valium proved not to be strong enough, so she started taking extra pills until they were gone. In panic, she turned to a high school friend and was introduced to Quaaludes, and she could take all of these she wanted. They took the anxiety away so beautifully and left such a hypnotic, peaceful feeling inside. She became addicted.

Pam was raised by her mother after her mother had gone through a painful divorce when she was three years old. She could remember vaguely the threats, fights, and early-morning escapes from the house with her mother when her father came home drunk and vicious. She remembered trembling the rest of the night, scared to death. She acquired her mother's anxiety and felt helpless so much of the time.

And so she did not trust herself or her decisions. She always had opposing feelings about things and ended up immobilized and anxious. She wouldn't let her mother out of her sight for a long time after her mother's divorce, and her mother grew very tired of that. So her "head" realized that she upset her mother by clinging so much; yet her "heart" was desperate for security. She felt helpless with the two persons inside in such conflict. She wanted to grow up, but was too insecure to do so. Her twisted relationship with self formed the basis of her anxiety.

As she grew older, any decision produced anxiety. She was afraid she would so anger her mother that her mother would abandon her if she made the wrong decision. On the other hand, she grew angry at herself for being so dependent. Even the smallest thing seemed to throw her into a turmoil. Her relationship with herself was broken. She had no trust of herself. This brokenness made her vulnerable to the chemical good feeling. It took away the awful anxiety and indecision and smoothed things out—until the demon took hold and she became addicted.

Addiction Growing Out of
Relationship with Others

Anger-fueled addiction. A person is vulnerable to addiction if there is a strong rebellious feeling inside. Often one or more persons have generated that anger inside by constant criticism. Instead of this anger turning inward (as in the guilt-related addiction), the person smolders with a desire to get even. There is a compulsion to hurt the person who has been critical. Drinking then takes on a rebellious flavor, as it did in Craig's life.

> Craig came from a good family. They had a good reputation in their small town, and his father and mother were very active in their church. But Craig's father, in his attempt to make sure Craig grew up right, was always on his back. Craig became defiant as a small child, and it was often his father's will against his. This usually ended up in an explosion and a harsh spanking for Craig. As he entered his teen years, his father started becoming very suspicious—accusing Craig of something if he was a few minutes late. Craig's smoldering defiance started breaking into hatred toward his father. One night, when he was only 14, he and a friend got hold of a fifth of vodka. As he took the first drink, something snapped inside his head. "I wish you could see me now, you - - - " he thought in anger. He felt at the moment that he had won. His father couldn't get to him now. He just didn't care! All the smoldering hatred seemed to erupt and left him feeling so powerful and high. He soon was to become a teenage alcoholic.

Craig was raised with his will pitted against his father's. His father saw him as an ungrateful, rebellious child and tried as hard as he could to change him. Craig saw his father as trying to break his will and felt that it was a fight to the finish. So much of his life became consumed with getting even with his father. That "anger-fuel" made him vulnerable to alcohol. It seemed as if alcohol could loosen that knot of hatred in his stomach and make him feel powerful. He knew that his drunkenness would hurt his father more than anything else he could do.

As with all bad spirits, his initial reason for drinking was soon no longer his reason for continuing. Drinking quickly became a demon in its own right, driving him with a compulsiveness that was even stronger than his rebelliousness. The desire for alcohol sat firmly in the driver's seat. Craig was now a possessed person, consumed with the constant desire for the next alcoholic evening.

Need-focused addiction. A person is vulnerable to addiction if there is a deep emptiness and yearning inside. A person who has lost a loved one or a person who feels a deep need for closeness but has lost hope for intimacy, is a prime candidate for addiction. The emptiness inside needs to be filled. Just ask Sharon:

> Sharon could twist her father around her finger. She was "daddy's girl" and could climb up on his lap, feeling close and warm. If she were sad, daddy would buy her things to cheer her up. She and her father were inseparable. When he was due home in the evening, she would stand at the window, looking for his car to pull into the driveway. But then one day, he didn't come home. She was only eight years old and couldn't understand why. They told her he had a heart attack, and she saw him once more at the funeral, but she was bewildered. Her world had been shattered, and she felt nothing but a deep hurt and emptiness inside. She cried herself to sleep many nights after that, yearning for him to come back. She never felt that closeness to her mother, but settled down to a somewhat normal teenage life. The horrible emptiness never left, however. She got married when she was 18 and had a child soon after and that helped. But as the child grew up and away from her and as her husband found his work more and more consuming, she found that a little wine mellowed things during the day. But it didn't take long for that "little wine" to turn into something harder and become more and more frequent. It started out warming that emptiness and fulfilling that yearning, but then she was hooked.

Sharon needed closeness and security. She tried to find it after her father died, but no one seemed to take his place. In fact, she did not trust men after that, fearing closeness. She feared losing them and being hurt again. So her emptiness was never touched and filled, making her vulnerable for something like alcohol to fill the emptiness. Her blocked relationships with others left her deep yearning unfulfilled. It seemed that alcohol was the only way she could find that good spirit again, but it turned out to be an evil spirit, destroying her marriage and her capacity to relate to her children.

Addiction Growing Out of the Loss of the Capacity to Relate

Apathy-grounded addiction. A person is also vulnerable to addiction if all hope for a good spirit within *any* relationship is gone because of the loss of one's capacity to relate. Such a person has lost hope for life without anyone or anything to believe in. Such a person has problems relating to God. Nothing is worth getting deeply excited about, and a detached cynicism is ever-present. Karl's apathy was all too apparent:

> Karl's favorite expression was a sarcastic, "Well, to hell with it then," accompanied by a shrug of his shoulders. If there was going to be conflict over anything, he would easily detach and feel that the whole thing was foolish and unimportant. He could be totally insulated at times and feel nothing at all. He learned this way to stop the pain when his drunken father cruelly slapped him around and beat him with whatever was handy. The beatings happened so often when he was young that he learned how to stop feeling anything. As he grew older, the smoldering anger was about the only thing that could slip through this insulation. It would come out as a subtle, cutting remark. Everyone was afraid of Karl. But there was one situation in which he could feel again. After he had enough liquor, the insulation would break down. He would pour out his feelings to anyone, usually ending up crying, bubbling over with emotion. But then he had to be extra vicious and sarcastic when he sobered up to cover up the breakthrough of feeling. Nevertheless, the emotional release did make him feel human again, and he got hooked on his weekend drunken sprees.

The loss of hope in Karl's life really meant that he had nothing to believe in. He saw relationships as hurtful and had so insulated himself that he could find nothing to get deeply excited about. He had so blocked his yearning that, except for the drunken slobbering, he did not feel anything. He was usually bored and apathetic, cynical about everything. He couldn't believe in a God who would allow his world to get into such a mess. He would savagely cut down any attempts to witness to him and talk about his salvation. "Those phony do-gooders," he would sneer. "Alcohol is the only spirit I'm going to believe in!"

In a sense Karl had found another god and had sold his soul to it. And our culture provides ample rationalizations to keep persons from facing addiction. "Just a bend of the elbow and things will be rosy again." "One more won't hurt." "I can stop any time I want to." "I deserve it after a long hard day's work." Or if the individual rationalizations are not enough, commercials provide idealizations that make addiction seem acceptable. Drinking is always associated with friends having a good time.

Breaking the Spirit

So, with a culture that provides the idealization and the "computer personality" that fits in with the insulating properties of drugs, what hope is there for the addict? The bad spirit involved is a difficult one to deal with because at first it closely imitates a good spirit—and then it gradually becomes more and more important to the person until it is in the driver's seat. Then it is a demon.

In dealing with addicts, there often seems to be no hope because of the extent to which they have sold their soul to the substance. They become hardened con artists and cannot be trusted. Promises and pretense come easy to them.

This bad spirit must be broken. But how? To begin, establish personal contact through a commitment to that person's soul. Then avoid getting sucked in and manipulated; avoid the games the addicts want to play. Pay no attention to excuses and promises—or even expressions of guilt and remorse. Confront the addicts and stay with them, following their emotions until you can break through, getting to the yearning. Allow the rage and hostility to surface until the hurt feeling emerges. Get to the original point of brokenness. Get them to see the demon and to name the bad spirit—to acknowledge that they are no longer free and need help.

For you see, the addict still has a soul. Somewhere, deep down, a caring word and loving contact can yet touch this person. For the yearning is still there, no matter how insulated it has become. The truth of the Word can still strike home. The Holy Spirit can still break through as you "speak the truth in love."

13

How to Deal

with Sexual "Demons"

Sexual demons are deep emotions and, as such, have power. Too often we have refused to acknowledge this power. This refusal to acknowledge the power of sexual emotions surfaced as a Puritan attitude on the one hand and later as a humanist attitude on the other. The Puritan attitude that repressed sexual feelings has given way to a more humanistic viewpoint that sexual expression is a natural part of every person's life. Both viewpoints have valid arguments, but what is often overlooked is that both viewpoints also have their demons.

The Puritan repressive attitude tended to produce sexual obsessions and deviant impulses. Sigmund Freud pointed out the demons that repression brought about. It was as if the person's "head" were trying to eliminate the "heart." But the repressed impulse did not go away. Instead it gathered fuel in the unconscious and would break loose in uncontrolled thoughts or behavior. The "heart" merely waited until it had sufficient power; then it took over through the obsessive or compulsive act. Repression turned out to be a bad spirit or false way to develop life and spirit. The demons aroused this way were sometimes violent and too often neurotic.

In an attempt to free the culture from such repressed "demons" and give greater freedom of expression, the humanistic viewpoint has also brought along its demons. This viewpoint, you will remember, sees a person as basically good. Sexual feelings are natural, and the person has the right to experience this pleasure in whatever setting he or she chooses as long as there is no harm to another person.

However, a person's sexuality goes much deeper than this and is a basic part of the yearning process of one's soul. In the humanistic attempt to "free up" sexual expression, this deep yearning becomes misplaced in shallow encounters. Sexual feelings then become detached from their depth, and sex becomes banal—without the mystery and excitement that are a part of the good spirit.

The demon then is apathy and impotency—not an impotence arising from Puritan guilt, but impotence arising from the "bedpost" syndrome. The person is detached, sitting on the bedpost, observing his or her own sexual activity and is not a part of his or her body at that moment. The demon is the anxiety over the ability to function and leads to an obsession for orgasm. The demon comes from making sexual expression a casual affair. The deep yearning is insulated, and the person is forced into an unfulfilling, surface expression.

The Deep Emotions

An individual has both surface and deep emotions. The surface emotions are part of the "head" or that person inside who steps back and observes how things are going. These are the passing emotions that are a part of more casual events and interactions of the day. A Dallas Cowboy football game on any given Sunday in the fall stirs up some emotion in me. I get excited watching the game, but the outcome does not really affect my deeper mood. And yet a few complimentary words from Kathy and that deeper mood is very much affected. That's feeling good all the way through.

The deeper emotions are not easily detached. Instead, they have roots in the deep yearning of the soul. As these rooting emotions reach into the soul, basic emotional sustenance is given to the whole energy system of a person.

A person's sexual drive has the power to deepen relationships in a beautiful way. Deep sexual yearning fulfilled in the good spirit of a marriage is priceless. The two persons never tire of each other, because the yearning comes from deep within the soul. The prospect of a weekend off somewhere together is an exciting prospect for Kathy and me, even after 20 years of marriage. Such love fulfilled is ever new and fresh —like a wellspring from deep down. This is God's gift to us for our spirits.

Sexual yearning is intertwined with other deep emotions. That is why hurt in this area arouses such powerful emotions. The effect of an affair is always demonic—unless the marriage relationship was completely broken anyway. Deep jealousy, bitterness, hatred, and an obsessive desire to know every detail are some of the forms the demon takes when there has been an affair. The loss of the fulfillment of this deep yearning (through death or breakdown of what had been a good relationship) produces an indescribable emptiness. Such a deep ache and the obsessive thoughts over the past close times produce some of the deepest pain I have ever encountered. I still remember Duane's deep moan:

> A deep moan, almost like that of a person about to die, came out of Duane's mouth. He was going through the process of divorce and was trying to tell himself that it was for the best. Suddenly he was gripped by memories of the incredible closeness he had felt with his wife only last winter. As they sat by the fireplace, sharing their hopes and dreams, they couldn't touch each other enough. The memories came in waves, and his moaning revealed the depth of his hurt. He would give anything at that moment to be close to her again—anything.

Duane's marriage had broken up with the involvement of a third party. He knew that his jealousy had helped push his wife away, but he never thought she would actually carry out her threat to call it quits. The pain and depression he felt were worse than anything he had ever experienced.

Is Sex Necessary?

Since one's sexual feelings are part of the deep emotions, is it possible for a person to be fulfilled without having a sexual partner? Attitudes within our culture suggest that everyone, married or not, has a right to sexual fulfillment. The term "sexually active" is an attempt to put a neutral label on sexual behavior—as if it were a natural experience that any person could have without consequence. But this attitude almost makes the sex act an objective event and not a subjective experience.

A person can experience deep closeness with another without overt sexual expression. And such "spiritual" closeness is far more fulfilling than a few minutes of sexual intimacy in some casual relationship. Spiritual closeness stays with the person and warms the soul. Casual sexual intimacy and the good feelings this generates leave almost as quickly as the orgasm is finished.

So, contrary to the propaganda of our culture, a person can be deeply happy and fulfilled without being "sexually active." The yearning of the soul for closeness with others can no doubt be deeply satisfied through a sexual relationship within the context of a deeply committed relationship. But the yearning can also be satisfied by the intimacy of emotional sharing without sexual activity. Sex is not the god that holds the key to happiness. Rather sex becomes one of the many ways a person can experience deep fulfillment. Sex is no more important, but no less important, than any of the other ways to experience depth in one's life.

In our marriage, sexual intimacy helps the depth of our good spirit—but only when the rest of our relationship is in order. Even our sexual encounters fail to be deeply satisfying if they do not flow from a spiritual closeness between us. If we are not in good spirits with each other, sexual activity is robbed of its depth and lasting warmth.

Since sexual feelings are part of our deep, mood-changing emotions, sexual intimacy has the power to help break through a bad mood in the spirit of marriage. It brings us back into physical contact and has the power to help bring back the good spirit. That is the beauty of the sexual feelings as they interplay with the other deep emotions to produce that spirit.

How Far to Go

So, how can a person determine the proper sexual expression? In a dating relationship how far should one go? With the realization that one's sexual feelings are part of the deep emotions, a good rule of thumb would seem to be: *The level of sexual arousal should match the depth of the relationship.* Deep sexual arousal on the first date just does not fit—nor does only holding hands after dating for a year.

Consider for a moment what happens when deep sexual arousal is experienced within a casual relationship. In the first place, the emotions produced are much too deep for the shallow relationship to handle. That's like putting 220 volt current through a motor wired for 110 volts. This overbalanced emotional arousal will usually end up destroying the relationship:

Betty had noticed Bob for some weeks at the singles bar. She had exchanged many glances with him, she found such eye contact exciting. There was a definite sexual attraction between the two of them. When he came over to talk to her, there was good feeling and energy between them. Their relationship really had potential. They talked and talked, finding each other interesting and easy to relate to. It seemed that they were meant for each other. They set up a date for the next weekend, and both looked forward to meeting again with high excitement. Again they found the magic together, and both found their deep loneliness starting to ebb. They needed each other. But then the demon struck! They went back to the bar on their third date for a few drinks. The yearning was so deep and the attraction so strong that they ended up at his apartment for the night. Betty awoke in the morning with a bad feeling inside. She looked at the unshaven, sleeping man next to her and felt a wave of revulsion go over her. "He was just using me," a loud voice spoke inside her head. "He's just like all the other men—just after what he can get." When Bob called the next evening, the magic was gone. All that was left was a polite coolness in Betty's voice and a vague promise to get back in touch some time.

A story like that is sad, but happens constantly. The deep yearning coupled with loneliness make sexual encounters highly attractive. These persons are often vulnerable to a bad spirit because of this loneliness. But the excitement and spirit derived from sexual intimacy then arouses the demons—emotions too powerful for the shallow relationship to handle. Feelings of being manipulated or used enter in, become powerful, and break the relationship. Then it becomes one big game, robbing the budding relationship of its opportunity to become a deep one.

In addition to being lonely, the persons involved now have another hurt. This hurt further insulates their deep emotions, reducing their capacity for deeply trusting anyone again. And as the feeling of being used grows, so does the loneliness and hopelessness. The demonic force of the "used" feelings weakens the potential for a good spirit again. With their deep feelings insulated, these persons become trapped in their own emotions and hurt, rationalizing with, "Well, what can you expect? All men will do that to you."

So, again, how do you know how far to go on a date? Perhaps the best gauge as to how much arousal is appropriate comes after the fact. If the closeness and deep good feelings persist when you wake up the next morning, the arousal apparently was appropriate. But if it is hard to face yourself or the other person the next morning, something is wrong.

However, before you tell yourself everything is OK, remember that the capacity of the human mind to rationalize is infinite. It is all too easy to quiet down or overlook that nagging feeling, especially if you have insulated your sexual feelings.

Shallowness vs. Commitment

In fact, the most common problem I encounter in the sexual area comes from taking such sexual feelings lightly. Since these are deeply-rooted emotions, making their expression casual arouses demons. When a person makes a surface emotion out of this deep one, then one of two things usually happens to the person: (1) either the person further insulates the deep emotions or, (2) the person becomes deeply committed in a relationship that was intended to be shallow.

Chad reflects this further insulation of his deep emotions:

> Chad was 35 and desperate! Sex was such an important part of his manhood, yet he had become impotent with his wife. Throughout high school and college he had been sexually active. A few years after getting married, he started having that old restless feeling. He would find himself playing the familiar game again, looking at every woman he met, judging whether she would be available or not. A surge of excitement would come with the challenge, followed by a gradual tiring of that woman after a half-dozen sexual encounters. The pattern repeated itself two or three times a year over the 10 years of his marriage. During the excitement phase he was also very potent with his wife, but lost interest in her when an affair wound down. Towards the end, having an affair seemed to be the only way to stir up his sexual feelings. A note of desperation set in. The game was getting old. And he was having more and more trouble with his sexual arousal.

Chad's demon finally overcame him. His affairs took on a more and more obsessive character, and he enjoyed them less and less. Actually, they just weren't that exciting anymore, so he was driven harder and harder to find that old excitement. His growing impotency became an obsession. It was all he thought about. Then finally his worst fears were realized: he became totally impotent with his wife.

So what happened to Chad? Years and years of displacing his sexual feelings and experiencing them outside of a deep relationship had taken its toll. They became more and more insulated—more and more a part of a big game—until they lost their deep energy. His sexual feelings were no longer connected with the deep yearning for love and closeness with others. So when the game got old, there was nothing deep to sustain his sexuality. His yearning was blocked from its sexual expression. At that moment the demon had won. Chad was totally incapable of sexual expression in a deep relationship.

Oh, yes, a bad spirit had been with him all the way. He had a beautiful rationalization for his affairs. He found that he was more attentive to his wife and that their sexual life was more exciting when one of his affairs was going on. So "for the good of his marriage," he would have another affair. As he accepted that rationalization, the bad spirit won the day.

He did regain his sexual potency, but only after going through "hell." His wife had lived in her own fantasy world and had succumbed to her own bad spirit by overlooking the innumerable clues of Chad's affairs. When he finally became impotent and desperate, she couldn't overlook it anymore and confronted him one evening. His desperation prompted him to admit the last affair he had. Then she had a demon! She became obsessed about what he had done, lashing out at him with each new detail.

Night after night, week after week they talked, wrestling with each of their demons, knowing only that they somehow wanted to stay together. They ripped open every detail of his affairs. Confession and forgiveness—like a chisel—broke through the wall. He was potent again with his wife. Chad's sexual feelings were finally rooted in his deeper yearning.

Admittedly, their marriage had lost something. There were many scars that took a long time to heal. Her trust in him is still not completely back, but a new relationship is growing. There is a deeper happiness in their lives now that had not been there for years. The yearning for each other is on the "right" track and their love for each other is now beautiful to see.

The other demon that can be aroused by taking sexual expression lightly is deep emotional commitment within a shallow relationship. In spite of her best intentions, Barbara became committed:

> Barbara was out of college and was working far away from where she had grown up. She had been hurt deeply several times with college relationships. So when she met George at work, she was content to keep it a more casual relationship with no commitments on either side. They became sexually involved fairly rapidly, prompted by the deep loneliness they both had. They carefully stayed away from any ties with each other. There would be no permanent commitments. Neither wanted to be hurt again. They got along well and were able to respect the freedom of the other, so the convenience of living together seemed to be a natural thing to consider. It seemed to be an ideal relationship. Both were getting their needs met, and it seemed to work out fine. But then the demons came! Barbara found herself getting emotionally involved after about six months of living together. One night after sex, she brought up the subject of marriage, but George just rolled over and said nothing. He wasn't interested. The next day, some of his habits started annoying her and she started picking at him. Then they started arguing over little things and over the next few months got more and more frustrated with each other. As things started deteriorating, Barbara became insanely jealous, accusing George of everything she could imagine. It got so bad that one night he beat her up, and she moved out—confused, hurt and completely unsure of herself.

So, what happened? Barbara had become emotionally committed to George, but he was not committed to her. Their "convenient" sexual arrangement had reached her deep feelings, but there was no place for these feelings to call home. So, once again, the message is clear: the level of sexual arousal should match the depth of the relationship. Whenever it does, the spirit has a chance to grow and flourish.

14

Divorced and Yet
in Good Spirits

Being divorced and being in good spirits do not seem to go together. The hurt and bitterness that accompanied the breakup of the marriage now sit as a cold lump in the person's stomach, keeping any deep good feelings from emerging. The only relief from the brokenness comes from focusing anger on the former spouse. So, can a divorced person be in good spirits again?

The answer is yes! Even though divorce represents a broken relationship and hence a broken spirit, good spirits can still be a part of the person's life. For there are still other relationships that can energize the person's spirit.

But, more importantly, it is even possible to work through the divorce so that it deepens a person's spiritual life. All things have the potential for enhancing one's spiritual life: "All things work together for good to those who love God!" (Rom. 8:28). So a person can be sick or can even be dying and be in good spirits. A person can experience financial crisis or have a child die and still be in good spirits! In the same way, a person can be divorced and be in good spirits.

Death and Renewal

Being in good spirits is to have one's relationships with self, others, and God open and deep. Going through a death in the family can turn the family members against each other in blame and unexpressed guilt, or it can be the catalyst for deep soul-searching and renewal of the family relationships. Terminal illness can get stuck in denial and repressed anger, or it can be the catalyst for the deepest sharing and soul-searching. All such experiences can create a good spirit if they are seen as opportunities for working on one's relationships.

Divorce represents the breakdown and death of the spirit of the marriage. It is often worse than losing a spouse through death. The presence of demonic emotions and the depth of self-doubt cry out for spiritual renewal. Many times one divorced person tries to renew the broken relationship, only to find the potential for restoring a good spirit between the divorced couple is no longer there. Attempts on the part of one party to restore contact are then met with suspicion and hostility, resulting in more hurt and brokenness. Sarah tried:

> Sarah still had hope deep down. Oh, she was well aware of the finality of the divorce proceedings, but something told her that she and Sam would some day find each other again. She thought of him all the time, alternating between hating him for his cruelty and critical outbursts and yearning for his closeness and familiar contact. So much of her energy was still wrapped up in Sam. She was hungry for any bit of information about him and started finding excuses for making contact with him. Sometimes it would be the familiar closeness when they talked on the phone—but then an argument would erupt and the hurt came rushing back. This would throw Sarah into a depression for days and keep her twisted and churned up inside. Both still had feelings for each other, but continued contact seemed to result only in more hurt.

The Demons of Divorce

For so many people, divorce does not mean the beginning of something new. So many feelings are usually left unresolved

—like breaking contact without being able to work through any of the powerful emotions that got stuck in the process. Those powerful emotions and the brokenness they represent are ripe for a bad spirit. Those emotions can so easily seek expression in a destructive way, ending up in more brokenness for the person.

One such bad spirit is *denial*. "Boy, I'm really better off without that relationship." "There was never really anything there when we got married." "The relationship just died. We grew apart and were no longer compatible." "There are plenty of other fish in the sea."

Denial allows the person to cover up and explain away the hurt and thus feel better for the moment. The process gives the person a better spirit, but it is evil because it leads to further destruction. The denied emotions do not go away, but are just further blocked from being expressed. Jan tried denial:

> Jan went through the divorce fairly calmly. For many years she had known that their marriage was no longer happy. Sure, it hurt when she found out about the other woman, but somewhere deep down she was not surprised. She had been yearning for the same thing herself. So she was civil about the whole thing, and the divorce went smoothly. She would shrug when asked what happened and reply, "Well, we just grew apart and lost interest in each other." Jan started dating again. But the moment she felt the beginnings of emotional involvement with a man, she would lose interest in him. Her capacity to form a deep relationship had been diminished. The emotions of her marriage were still stuck inside her, blocked by her denial of them. So she would end up telling herself again that she did not need anyone.

Another bad spirit that shows up around divorce time is *blame*. It becomes all "her fault." "Boy, did she ever fool me. I should have known that she couldn't be trusted." "All he did was lie to me. Everything he said was a lie." "So he thought he could get away with it. I'll make him hurt." "She'll be sorry she tried to make me look like a fool."

Bart put all the blame on his wife:

Bart was the "innocent" party. He was the one who claimed to want to work it out, but his wife went ahead with the divorce. Bart just knew that another party was involved and towards the end of their marriage accused her almost daily of having an affair. He would find suspicious items and read things into his wife's actions. He started following her at unusual times and kept up his detective work long after the divorce was final. He would drive around her apartment, letting her know he was there. It looked as if he were living to harass her.

Bart chose to put the blame on his wife for the marriage breaking up, and as a result ended up with a demon. Long after they were divorced, he was driven to check up on her. She was in his thoughts daily, and he grew to hate her. His hatred seemed to consume his life.

That's really what a demon is: a person's deep emotion that has become locked into a destructive path. Such emotions turn back on the person and begin driving the person's life. Bart's hatred was, in the final analysis, his own problem. He was stuck with the hatred and couldn't work past his obsession to get even. He ended up a pathetic person, always wanting to talk about "her" and what she had done to him.

And Bart's demon did not stop there. He did meet another person and started dating. She was a good listener, and he talked at length about how his former wife had hurt him. Their relationship grew, and Bart started feeling new life begin.

But then the demon struck! They were out for a romantic evening, and everything seemed to be going quite well. But Bart started getting a strange anxious feeling, as if something were about to happen. He was a little edgy with the conversation, finding things to criticize in his date's behavior. She started getting annoyed and felt trapped by his constant picking. So she stopped looking at Bart and started looking around the restaurant. Her eyes met a handsome man sitting alone, and instinctively she returned his smile. Bart jerked as he saw the warm exchange and immediately "knew" she had something "going" with him. His old jealousy and hurt flared up inside him and his eyes grew cold. "So, you'd rather be with him," Bart accused.

And so ended the potential relationship Bart was trying to establish. He pounced on any hint that the woman he was with was not true to him. His biting accusation made a new relationship difficult. Bart was somewhat incapable of a deep relationship at that point. Anyone would have a hard time getting past Bart's demons!

Yet divorce does not have to end up producing demons in the persons involved. There are two paths at this point, one destructive and the other creative. In the destructive path, the person tries to cover up or soothe the hurt by huge doses of denial or blame. The person initially feels relief, but is then stuck with unresolved deep feelings. The hurt was smoothed over, but no deep healing occurred. And that deep hurt is now free to rear its ugly head in future situations. You then have a bitter person.

The Creative Path

Thank God there is another path, the creative path. There is a creative time during and right after the divorce proceedings when healing can take place, when *the brokenness can no longer be hidden*. This path is more painful, but it is a path toward depth and openness. Here are six steps along that path:

1. See the divorce like a death. Assume that it is final. This allows you to face the brokenness in all of its pain and to get a clear starting point. If there is any hope for renewal of the marriage relationship, this is what must first happen. It's like losing your life to regain it.
2. Acknowledge the hurt to yourself. Recognize that the hurt comes from having deeply loved. Picture your emotions as being raw and wounded, needing care and attention to be healed.
3. Stay with the hurt. Let the wound stay open and heal from the inside. Recognize that it takes time for your emotions to heal. The deeper the relationship, the greater the hurt. Give your mourning time for expression.

4. Keep from pretending to yourself and others that everything is fine. Once acknowledged, the pain becomes less significant.
5. Don't rebound. Resist the temptation to focus your feelings on another person to soothe the hurt and loneliness. See this as a creative time for soul-searching and personal growth.
6. Then, when your emotions are ready, recognize that some emotional adjustment is needed. The emotional outlets you had in your spouse now need to be rechanneled. New outlets need to be developed in other people and in new activities.

For a person going through a divorce, a context of acceptance and understanding is crucial. The good spirit within the body of Christ can provide this context in which God's love is expressed. The divorced person's broken spirit is in the open. This is a time that the person can be touched and affirmed.

How are new channels of emotional expression opened? How is this emotional adjustment made? New and open relationships with others (and the good spirit developed in them) are needed at this time. The Christian community can provide opportunity for honest emotional expression—for soul-searching in a safe context, relatively free from bad spirits, so that the person can find out who they are again. The person going through the divorce probably does not know self anymore, since this person's identity was inseparably tied up in the marriage relationship.

This is not the time to pass judgment. A broken spirit is not a bad spirit! The spirit of the Christian community at this critical time can allow the person to feel and express the brokenness. Friends can reach this person so that the torn and mangled emotions can be healed.

The creative path is not an easy one, nor a short one. Openness, sharing and forgiveness allow the divorced person to heal from the inside out. And by taking this creative path, the person can have a good spirit again.

15

Working with

the Family Spirit

A new baby is brought into the world. The child has the potential as one of God's children to develop a life filled with good. But this potential has to be unlocked, and the child cannot do it herself. The deep yearning is there, and the capacity for good relationships and good spirits is intact. But for her capacity to be tapped, she must first be affirmed by others outside herself. She must be loved by someone before she has the ability to love herself and others.

The child's experience of love is concrete—in the cuddling, playing, laughing, protecting, and other forms of contact of a caring parent. Then the child comes alive—kidding back, laughing, and becoming a sheer delight of emotional expressiveness. You can almost see the good spirit being born within this child.

But without loving contact that affirms the child, this potential for good spirits remains dormant, waiting, perhaps forever, for affirmation that would bring the good spirit to life. Deep within all who have never been affirmed is still that hope and yearning—sometimes so repressed that it is scarcely recognizable. But it is still there.

The Place of Discipline

And so children need *love*—not the "love" that gives them everything, but the love that really touches them and allows for deep, fulfilling contact. Part of this love is discipline. Love is certainly not leaving a child alone to do what she wants or giving in to the child's every request. Rather, love is the building-block of the relationship with the child. Proper discipline shows a depth of caring for the child's life. And the child grows and develops into a healthy personality through the creative interplay of "speaking the truth in love" within the context of a good spirit between parent and child.

It is tempting to overdiscipline the child out of concern that the child know what is right. Placing the boundaries too rigidly forces the child to react to the external rules, setting the stage for problems the child will have with authority at a later age. The child will either adopt a strategy to please everyone, or the child will rebel. Either way, the child is left with a poor self-image, feeling that there is no way to please the parent:

> Craig was the ideal child. He would say, "Yes, sir," and would never talk back, doing anything that was asked. He seemed quite anxious at times, however, almost too eager to please. And if he did not do something exactly right and his father, as usual, would quickly point it out, he would get depressed about it and think back over his failure again and again. Perhaps it was because his father had always reminded him of things he did wrong and would never let him forget.

St. Paul advises parents not to be too harsh on their children, lest the children lose their spirit. Constant criticism is initially effective, and the resultant anxiety produces immediate results in the child. But, like a bad spirit, as the child grows older, it leads to greater destruction in the depression or rebellion. Resisting the temptation for quick results by a heavy hand, parents can confront and discipline with patience and love. Letting the child know right and wrong firmly and consistently is essential, and force is sometimes necessary. But then following through to build a deeper relationship is also essential. The spirit of forgiveness must also be ever-present.

Complete permissiveness is just as bad as rigid discipline. It is tempting to placate and give in to the child. This bad spirit of giving in seems to make things run smoothly in the family, giving the appearance of a good spirit for a time. But, like harshness, this permissiveness does not help build relationships. It becomes an easy excuse to put the child off without giving attention to what he or she is struggling with. The child is left without a good sense of boundaries—of right and wrong. Such a child often gets in trouble in order to find some boundaries:

> Joe was always asking questions. His parents were busy with their separate jobs and their many social activities. His mother would only half-listen to what he had to say and then give an ambiguous reply. When Joe wanted something, all he had to do was talk long enough and he would end up getting his way. Whenever he was told that he could not do something, he would put up such a fuss that his parents would give in to have some peace. As Joe grew older, he had a poor sense of boundaries. He was not considerate of others and would do most anything that he felt he could get by with. He just assumed that he could talk his way out of anything.

And so in the intricate interplay of love and discipline the relationship between parent and child grows. As the resulting tension helps deepen the relationship, the spirit of the family grows. But if the inevitable tension is either squashed by parental authority or insulated by permissiveness, demons take over.

The Marriage Relationship

So often, it seems, the precursor of problems within the parent–child relationship are problems within the relationship between parents. And basic disagreements on childrearing seem to lie at the heart of so many problems between spouses:

> Jill was never allowed to talk back to her parents. Especially when her father told her to do something, discussing it

with him was unthinkable. She was raised to respect what he said and keep her reactions to herself. George came from a completely different background. He would regularly voice his opinion to his parents, and they would listen to what he had to say, frequently giving into him. He saw nothing wrong with "talking back." Jill and George were married and were very happy for the first four years. But then the children came. The first time their young son showed signs of rebellion, Jill expected George to come down hard. But when George found the "no" somewhat cute and seemed to encourage it, Jill blew up! *A child has to learn from the beginning who is boss,* Jill thought and couldn't understand George's reaction. That was the beginning of endless arguments and disagreements between them. In fact, Jill started overcompensating for what she considered George's permissive attitude and came down twice as hard. George, in turn, overcompensated for what he considered Jill's harsh discipline and came to the child's rescue. It seemed to get worse and worse over the years, and the family spirit weakened.

So often a basic disagreement between the parents shows up in the child's relationship with self. So often such a child gets conflicting messages from the parents, thus having trouble getting things together inside self. One of the persons inside the child identifies with father and the other with mother. If the parents' relationship is not together, it is hard for the child to get "heart" and "head" together!

In the above example, the child's "head" would most likely identify with Jill, since she was the disciplinarian of the family. But the "heart" would identify with George who liked to joke around and play with the child. These two persons inside the child mirror the relationship of the parents. Thus the child would have opposing impulses and would have a struggle with self, ending up a problem child.

If this is the case, the way to help this child is to have the parents shift roles. In the above case George would become the disciplinarian and Jill would be the "soft" person:

At first it seemed corny to them, but since things had gotten desperate, George and Jill agreed to switch roles. Their child was now a teenager and had become impossible to control.

Any time Jill would question him, he would blow up and stomp out of the room. If she would refuse him the car, he would disappear and not return until all hours of the night. He would literally act "crazy" at Jill's attempts at disciplining him, and their fights had become a daily, bitter dispute. He had even put his foot through the door in anger when Jill asked him where he had been. George, on the other hand, felt so helpless. He knew something was badly wrong, but blamed it on the harshness of his wife, just as she blamed it on his permissive attitude. To see the problem as one of their relationship was a new way of looking at it.

Their teenager was not a happy person. He really did not know why he reacted so violently when his mother would get on him for something. All he knew was that an overwhelming sense of injustice flew all over him, and his first reaction was to fight back. But then, after he blew up, he would feel guilty and worthless. He blamed himself for his parents' problems and even thought of suicide. He assumed that they would be a lot happier without him. But, try as he might, his good intentions of being different toward his mother blew apart the very next time she demanded something of him. He just went crazy again!

It took rehearsal and preparation to pull off the role shift. It sounded simple in theory, but for George to begin to notice things and to follow through with some discipline went against his nature. It was just too easy to let things slip by and not make waves. So it took effort on his part to set the limits and to follow through when his son stepped over the line. But Jill's role shift was no easier. She had to develop the attitude that George's way of handling things was OK. She had to back off and shrug off things she noticed. And, above all, Jill had to let George notice things himself. If she were to prompt him and get on his back for not seeing something, nothing would really have changed. Their son would have seen Jill as the one behind the discipline and would have reacted the same way.

So, armed with determination, they successfully made the role shift. George was able, with many slips, to keep on top of things, and Jill was able, also with many slips, to back off and trust George's reactions. And the result was astounding. As they shifted roles, their son's "head" and "heart" came together. He would not like what his father said to him, but he did not feel this crazy, powerful demonic desire to rebel that was present when his mother would discipline him.

In shifting roles, Jill and George found a new way of relating to each other and a new insight into what the other had felt over the years. They continued the habit of talking and sharing with each other that they had begun. With their relationship better, the whole family spirit improved, and many of the demons were chased out.

The dominant element in the family spirit lies in the relationship between the parents. If that spirit is good, chances are the family spirit will be good. Likewise, if the spirit between the parents breaks down, it becomes a force that can destroy the family spirit.

The stage for such breakdown is usually set by the loss of daily contact needed to sustain relationships. As communication breaks down, emotions get stuck and moods start plaguing the family. Television with its passive communication and the come-and-go life-styles of family members start putting cracks in family communication. In this brokenness, the parents' relationship can turn into a power struggle.

Beyond the Power Struggle

Jane was tired of being the understanding one and giving in all the time. Karl was deeply involved in building up his business and seemed to come home later and later. So Jane felt herself stuck with taking care of the children and the house after she got home from work. She did not want to become a nagging wife, so she kept these feelings of being used by the family to herself. But as she found herself stuck night after night with the care of the family, those feelings grew stronger and stronger. So she tried guilt and started making little comments when Karl would come home and ask if he could help: "That's OK, I'm used to doing it all myself anyway." Karl felt the sting and then a helplessness came over him. "She just doesn't understand how much energy I have to put into work," he thought to himself. But he would swallow this thought and try to help out with a heavy feeling. After hundreds of such comments, Karl started feeling powerless at home. It seemed that nothing he could do was right for Jane, and he felt himself giving in to her all the time. So he started silent warfare tactics. He stopped asking her if he could help, and the first cutting comment she made, he would drop what he was doing and go turn on the TV. That made her furious, so she stepped up her side of the battle. As she escalated her cutting comments, he escalated his silent treatment until Karl and Jane were deadlocked in the power struggle.

Such a power struggle results in family disharmony. It not only goes on between husband and wife, but spreads to a struggle between parents and children, and between the children. It is a way of relating and a way of exercising one's will against another, but there is usually a bad spirit involved. A child, for example, accidentally finds a power lever by acting a certain way that turns the parents against each other. The child feels powerful and "enjoys" this ability to manipulate. But after doing this again and again, demons get aroused in the family spirit, as the parents' fights over the child get more and more destructive.

Power struggles are really attempts to manipulate the family spirit. They come from a lack of trust that one's needs will be met by the natural concern from other members of the family. The manipulation increases with its success (as is the case for all evil spirits), arousing demons as the other family members begin to feel manipulated and retaliate. Then bigger and bigger guns have to be brought in until full-scale warfare breaks out within the family.

So, to reverse the escalation, basic changes in family habits have to be made. The power struggle is really a breakdown in trust and understanding. The issue or problem involved makes little difference. It may be money, housework, the curfew for a child, or disciplining a child. If the family communication produces an automatic clash, little tends to get solved and the demons hang around for the kill.

To eliminate the power struggle both sides must seek reconciliation. The two family members may have basically different ideas, but the crucial difference is in the spirit in which these views are aired. To give an opinion with the intention of manipulating the situation or of exerting one's power within the family escalates the power struggle. On the other hand, to give the very same opinion with the intention of searching together for a way of handling the situation brings the family closer together. With such a spirit of forgiveness and reconciliation, anything, no matter how difficult, can result in a deeper relationship between the family members—even if the problem remains unresolved. Without this spirit of reconciliation the same crisis will only cause more hardened feelings and greater family disunity.

Breaking Down the Walls

Work on the family spirit must be top priority—especially in view of the cracks in the family structure that so easily occur as a result of TV and come-and-go life-styles. And how do you go about working on the family spirit? You do the same thing that you would with any other spirit: develop a deeper understanding of the other persons. This is the spirit of forgiveness and of reconciliation—to take time to understand the other person, even when that person has been hurtful to you. This is the stuff that breaks down walls within the family and allows for deeper feelings to be expressed.

A good way to begin work on the family spirit is to set a time aside each day for family conversation. Initially finding time to get together will be difficult, but finding time is merely a matter of priorities. If the family sees the importance of spending the time together, then it can happen. It may take some force at first to get it accomplished, but parental power used in this fashion is well worth it. Forcefully turning off the

TV set or forcefully arranging schedules so that everyone is home for supper is the only way to get the habit started.

As the family learns to converse with each other, family spirit is strengthened. The spirit then becomes the motivation for being together more often. Then it no longer becomes a struggle to get everyone together. Such a family enjoys being together. The family, like a person, can be in good spirits again!

However wonderful it is to be in good spirits yourself, it is multiplied many times over with a whole family in good spirits. It is God's yearning that we should be in good spirits—that we love one another, as God loves us.